FIGHT

*50 meditations on faith
that keeps swinging*

Kory M. Capps

From the Fray Publishing
8103 Stonefield Way
Tampa, FL 33635

www.fromthefray.com

Dedicated to my oldest, Karter.

You are a young man that stays in the ring, no matter the challenge.

You embody the heart and message of this book and

I'm deeply proud of you, son.

Acknowledgments

To Elizabeth, my beautiful wife, best friend, and faithful battle-buddy: Your unwavering support and encouragement mean the world to me, beyond what words can fully convey. Thank you for journeying alongside me in crafting this book, offering your invaluable insights, and providing your guidance. You are the definition of strong. I'm amazed by your gritty, rugged faith. I love you.

To Jonny and Hudson: In more ways than I can express, you have taught me to fight, to keep getting up, to never quit. I love you both. To my baby girl, Adele: "Little," you inspire me with your fierce spirit, protective heart, and relentless joy. You are truly a fighter. Your encouragement throughout the writing process, your inspiring creativity, and the way you celebrate reaching the finish line with me mean the world. I love you.

To my Mom and Dad, thank you for your love, encouragement, and support through the years. You epitomize the essence of this book. You are the grittiest people I know. You have fought the fight; you have kept the faith. I love you.

To my brothers, Tony, Jeff, and Kelly: This title might lead you to expect a tale about four brothers coming up together, wrestling, camping, biking, road-tripping, suffocating each other with couch cushions, laughing, playing Dutch Blitz, and perhaps leaving someone—whose name will remain unspoken—out in the snow in their underwear on Christmas day. And while this isn't that book, we are where we come from. Each of you has shaped me in ways that continue to influence not only my life today but also the undercurrent of this and other projects. I am certain, I have not thanked you enough. I love you all.

To my fellow warrior shepherd in the ministry trenches, Bill Mesaeh: It's humbling to see our "From the Fray" vision take shape after all these years. Your investment in my life and your influence on my work and ministry are invaluable. My brother, stay the course, and never forget: "we give hope to men and keep none for ourselves." I love you.

Once again, a big thanks to everyone on the Fiverr team who worked on this project. Special thanks to Goran T., my go-to publishing manager, who oversaw the cover, and manuscript. Lastly, thanks to my Ingram Spark team for consistently delivering excellent publishing work. I'd like to give a special shout-out to Ben Gass, whose exceptional support has been invaluable on multiple projects, including this one.

Table of Contents

Introduction

Fight the good fight of faith.
(1 Timothy 6:12)

After twenty-one years of professional fighting, an undefeated record, and fifteen major world championships, Floyd Mayweather Jr. said, "boxing is easy, life is much harder." I can't speak to a career in the ring, but I do know that the battles we wage as human beings— whether as spouses, parents, employees, or friends—are just as real and sometimes even more rigorous than a boxing match.

In the ring, victory might be claimed within a defined timeframe, but the battles we face as individuals extend far beyond any ring or arena. For me, the wounds stemming from these life battles— whether relational, emotional, or spiritual—cut deeper into my soul than any broken bone ever could. Perhaps you can relate.

This is precisely why fight language is a fitting description of life. It is also the explanation for the old-fashioned fistfight being a prism through which to see faith. But how is it a lens for faith? What God says and what we feel rarely line up. God's Word says he is working for our good, yet we may wonder how it can be true as we watch our family members suffer, our health deteriorate, or our loved ones die.

God's Word says we are clean and forgiven; we feel guilty and unworthy. God's Word says we are chosen and accepted; we feel lonely and rejected. The fight of faith pushes past our emotions to what God says. This doesn't just happen; we have to fight for it.

The fight of faith is also a battle against our greatest adversaries— Satan, sin, death, and hell. These eternal enemies pose the gravest threat to our well-being, whether we recognize it or not. They threaten to unravel us and our only hope to conquer them lies outside ourselves in Jesus Christ. He confronts each of these threats through his life, death, and resurrection, effectively removing each from harming us.

We battle to believe what Jesus has done for us; this is how we overcome (1 Jn 5:5, Rev 12:11). To put on the armor of God is to be clothed and hidden in what Christ has done for us (Eph 6:10-20, Is 59:16-17); it is to rest in his finished work. The gospel, the good news of Jesus' death and resurrection, is how we fight—we press into it, trust it, believe it, hope in it, return to it, cling to it, and strive to never let it go.

Any good fighter must condition, train, hone their skills, and learn from their losses. When every night is fight-night, we must be ready to go. Any good faith training regimen will include these five things:

1. *Condition, Condition, Condition-* Fighting takes training, practice and rigor. Step into the ring with no conditioning, your downfall is certain. The fight of faith requires mastering the mechanics of hearing God's Word, pressing his promises into our souls, and holding onto them with all our might (Rom 10:17, Heb 10:23, 1 Cor 15:2). Doing this intentionally, repeatedly, and strategically conditions us for war (1 Cor 9:26).

2. *No Matter What, Keep Your Hands Up-* One author said that "life is war, that's not all it is, but it is always that." The battle is always on for the Christian. A punch in the face is always just around the corner and the enemy's "opportune time" is the moment we put our hands down (Lk 4:13). Peter's call to vigilance is a call to remember life is a cage match (1 Pet 5:8). The moment our hands come down is the moment we are getting dominated. Keep your hands up.

3. *Get Up Again and Again and Again-* You're going to get your nose broken, take heart—it means you are in the fight! Paul pointed to the scars on his body from following Jesus as signs of his battle worn faith (Gal 6:17), it's no different for you. When you get smoked, get back up, keep swinging, don't lay

down. Internalize Micah's fighting spirit: "though I fall, I will rise" (Mic 7:8) and realize that it has nothing to do with how many times you get dropped, it's all about how much you get back up (Prov 24:16).[1] The grit of getting on your feet over and over again develops the muscles of faith, it engages the discipline of repentance, and it pushes us back to the gospel. Always get up, always.

4. *Trust Your Corner Team*- While it may appear that someone is in the ring alone, in reality there is an entire community surrounding them and a corner team coaching them. "Don't drop your hands!" "Move, Move, Move!" "Go for the body!" Listen to their guidance and heed their instruction, they see things you don't and they bring perspective that's needed to weather every round. Further, they are there to pick you up, wipe your sweat and blood, heal up your wounds, and tell you to keep pushing (Eccl 4:9-10, Heb 3:12-14). Winning a fight is never a solo endeavor; trust your corner team.

5. *Fight Like Hell*- The stakes are high; we are fighting for our lives. The only way to fight hell is to fight like hell. Hell doesn't quit, darkness never lets up, it's ever-vigilant, always growing stronger, always getting more strategic, always coming. That's how we have to fight—with rage like the evil one, perseverance like our sin, tenacity like our conscience, and unquenchable fire like hell. There's too much on the line to enter the arena in any other way. Christ's battle rigor won our salvation, ours is the fight to continue believing, trusting, and obeying him at any cost.

My dear friends, we're in the fight of our lives, and if you're anything like me, you could also use all the help you can get. I won't pretend to have all the answers here; I've spent more time on the mat than on my feet. Yet, it's on the ground where I have learned the most about the fight; in fact, many of these reflections stem from the gasping lungs, broken noses, and black eyes that life has thrown me.

In this intense battle of life, you are not alone. My prayer is that

---

[1] Unless otherwise noted, all biblical quotations are from the ESV.

these pages strengthen you, increase your spiritual resolve, and provide strategic insight for the fight of faith. We got work to do. Let's get after it.

God's Military Campaign Against Death

The fight of faith is a fight to the death. And even then, the battle is not over. We've all been there, standing helpless and distraught as we watch death take what we love from us. It's an unspeakable reality that we rage against and work feverishly to overcome, but always without success. It's an enemy far beyond our capabilities—a foe that compels us to look beyond ourselves.

Death, this formidable adversary of humanity, looms large throughout history and is often depicted as an indomitable force before which all must eventually succumb (Rom 5:12-14; 1 Cor 15:26). However, there is remarkable biblical hope in relation to our mortality. According to the words of Paul, the coming of Christ signaled the "abolishment of death" and revealed the essence of life and immortality through the gospel (2 Tim 1:10).

On two occasions, we witness Jesus shedding hot tears when faced with the horrors of death. The well-known Bible verse "Jesus wept" occurs in this context (Jn 11:35). It's important to recognize that in these moments, the heart of Christ was filled not only with grief but also with turmoil, holy rage, and a deep determination to confront death (John 11:33, 38).

We see the same in the Garden of Gethsemane, where Jesus once again confronted the specter of death. It was there that his sweat mingled with blood and he prayed with "loud cries and tears" (Lk 22:44; Heb 5:7).

The gospel is a resounding proclamation of how God, the fierce Warrior, wages a relentless campaign against death. It is through the gospel, the sacrificial death and triumphant resurrection of Jesus

Christ, the God-man, that death itself is ultimately vanquished. Jesus fearlessly confronted death head-on, willingly embracing its clutches, only to dismantle it from within. In an astonishing act, this mighty conqueror was brought to his knees by the humble Nazarene.

At the cross, death arrogantly believed it could retain its hold on Jesus, swallowing him with the same insatiable greed it exhibits towards any mortal. Yet, death was incapable of imprisoning him (Acts 2:23-28). The tomb was conquered when the God-man arose, leaving death in ruins.

As Jesus cast off the burial garments that bound him, he emerged victorious, standing triumphantly over the empty tomb. Just as the great whale could not retain Jonah in its belly, so too was the grave compelled by the omnipotent hand of God to expel his Son.

The consequence of Christ's death and resurrection was the bestowal of the gifts of life and immortality. Not only was death obliterated, but humanity was granted the priceless immunity from its clutches. Immortality, a divine attribute reserved solely for God, became an extraordinary gift delivered through the gospel.

The gospel imparts an imperishable, incorruptible, and everlasting life, mirroring the quality of the Triune existence. This incredible news reveals that God, in his relentless pursuit of victory over death, has bestowed upon us a life free from its dominion.

Christ became a man to become a warrior, battling against everything that jeopardizes our eternal well-being. This concept is emphasized in the New Testament (Col 2:13-15; 1 Jn 3:8).

> *Since therefore the children share in flesh and blood, he himself likewise partook of the same things, that through death he might destroy the one who has the power of death, that is, the devil, and deliver all those who through fear of death were subject to lifelong slavery. (Heb 2:14-15)*

The coming of Jesus is the best news for us as we all must walk through the valley of the shadow of death, because through him, that valley will remain just that—a shadow. It will not have the final word.

The gospel reveals God as a mighty Warrior, with Jesus magnifying the splendor of God's martial strength and passion through his incarnation and cross. My friends, God is a fierce warrior who fights through death for you and me.

The Considerate God

If you want to know what God is like, you look to Jesus. What Jesus says, does, and feels reflects what God says, does, and feels. Looking through this lens, one cannot help but be profoundly moved by the way Jesus interacts with people.

As both fully God and fully man, he flawlessly embodies true humanity and true deity, unveiling God's very nature to us while also setting the standard for what a human being should be. In Jesus, we witness the brilliance of God's glory and the completeness of his divine essence (Heb 1:3; Col 1:19).

God's engagement with humanity is marked by profound consideration and compassion. Jesus, as the embodiment of God's love, exemplifies this in every encounter. He listens attentively to people's stories, shares meals with the outcasts, and even touches those suffering from frightening diseases, demonstrating that God is not distant or indifferent but intimately involved in our lives (Mk 1:40-42).

The gospel accounts recount how Jesus generously gave his time to those in need. He healed the blind, the paralyzed, and the sick, expressing his deep concern for their pain and questions. Jesus is not a stoic deity but a God who empathizes with our human struggles and sorrows.

Moreover, Jesus is not only concerned with the spiritual well-being of people but also with their physical needs. He miraculously multiplies bread and fish to feed the hungry crowds, showing that God is deeply attentive to our physical hunger and sustenance (Mk

6:30-44). The act of providing food demonstrates that God's love is practical and that he cares for the daily needs of his children.

In one particular account, Jesus encounters a woman who had been suffering from a hemorrhage for twelve years (Mk 5:25-34). Her desperate faith leads her to touch the hem of his garment, believing that even the slightest contact with Jesus would bring healing.

When Jesus perceives that power has gone out from him, he stops and seeks the woman. Instead of rebuking her for touching him, he tenderly addresses her as "daughter" and commends her faith, assuring her of his healing care. This display of compassion and personal attention reveals that Jesus values and cares for each individual intimately, acknowledging our unique struggles and needs.

Furthermore, Jesus' interactions with grieving families exhibit his profound empathy and understanding of human pain and loss. When Jesus raises the daughter of Jairus from the dead, he cracks open a window into the very heart of God (Mk 5:35-43).

In this story, we witness Jesus' deep sensitivity and attentiveness to the fear and desperation of the girl's parents. He responds to their heartfelt pleas with care and immediate action. With words of comfort, he breathes life into the lifeless child, astounding everyone present.

What follows after the miracle is remarkable. Jesus instructs them not to disclose the miracle to others and advises them to give the girl something to eat. At first glance, this may seem puzzling. After witnessing the miraculous restoration of life, the thought of sustenance might be the last thing on their minds.

However, it was not an afterthought for Jesus, but a display of his remarkable consideration and practical kindness. In this simple act of ensuring the girl had something to eat, we glimpse the heart of God—a God who not only restores life but also cares about the everyday needs of his people. His compassion is not limited to the extraordinary; it extends to the mundane aspects of our existence. It shows us that God's love is not abstract or distant; rather, it is tangible, practical, and deeply personal.

These stories, and many like them, paint a beautiful and comprehensive picture of Jesus as the embodiment of God's compassion, love, and practical care. His interactions with people reveal a God who is deeply moved by our struggles, who listens to our cries, and who meets our needs with tender consideration.

In Jesus, we find the perfect balance of deity and humanity—a Savior who not only saves us from condemnation but also restores and nurtures our creatureliness. Reader, his meticulous care for each individual in these stories conveys his posture towards us, toward you. Take heart, he is profoundly aware of you.

The Danger of the Cross and the Safety it Affords

As tradition has it, George Orwell once said, "we sleep soundly in our beds because rough men stand ready in the night to visit violence upon those who would do us harm." Safety has always been provided to us by others who embrace danger on our behalf, whether we are referring to the military, the police, or firefighters. This principle remains steadfast.

In the cross, we encounter this same paradox—the concept of enduring danger to ensure safety. As we touch the heart of this mystery, we come face to face with the ultimate expression of divine sacrifice and love: Jesus Christ. Through his ministry and the culmination of his sacrifice on the cross, Christ willingly traversed the treacherous path of danger to secure for us a refuge of eternal safety.

The juxtaposition of danger and safety within the context of Christ's mission defies rationality. How could an act of enduring danger lead to our ultimate safety? The answer lies in the nature of Christ's sacrifice—the laying down of his life to vanquish the very danger that threatened our existence. This divine calculus baffles the human mind but ignites the soul with awe and gratitude.

The Bible speaks of a Savior who willingly embraced danger to ensure our eternal safety. In Isaiah 53:3, we learn that he was "despised and rejected by men, a man of sorrows and acquainted with grief." He endured the rejection and hostility of those he came to save, willingly walking into the danger of a fallen world.

On the night of his betrayal, Jesus went to the Garden of Gethsemane, where he faced imminent danger and prayed, "Father, if you are willing, remove this cup from me. Nevertheless, not my will, but yours, be done" (Lk 22:42). In that moment, he accepted the peril of arrest, trial, and crucifixion to secure our redemption.

The cross epitomizes the profound nature of Christ's sacrifice and its relationship to our safety. The cross symbolizes Christ's triumph over sin and death, transforming a place of apparent danger into the gateway of eternal safety.

John Stott beautifully articulated this paradox, saying, "the essence of sin is man substituting himself for God, while the essence of salvation is God substituting himself for man." Let's think together on twenty concrete ways the cross produces safety for us.

1. *Atonement:* Our sin handled through Christ's sacrifice.
2. *Redemption:* Liberation from the bondage of sin.
3. *Forgiveness:* Removal of the guilt and consequences of sin.
4. *Justification:* Declared righteous before God through faith.
5. *Reconciliation:* Repair of broken relationship with God.
6. *Adoption:* Inclusion into God's family as his children.
7. *New Identity:* Transformation into a new creation in Christ.
8. *Freedom:* Liberation from the tyranny of the flesh.
9. *Victory over Death:* Assurance of life beyond the grave.
10. *Peace with God:* Removal of enmity through Christ's death.
11. *Cleansing:* Purification from the defilement of sin.
12. *Rescue from Darkness:* Transfer into the kingdom of light.
13. *Eternal Inheritance:* Assured of God's promises.
14. *Empowerment:* Access to the Holy Spirit's strength.
15. *Healing:* Restoration of spiritual and emotional wounds.
16. *Hope:* Certainty of Christ's return and God's kingdom.
17. *Union with Christ:* Intimate fellowship with the Savior.
18. *Security in Trials:* God's presence during challenges.
19. *Community:* Belonging to a fellowship of believers.
20. *Eternal Safety:* Assurance of God's presence forever.

The cross, a symbol of suffering and death, becomes the bridge that connects us to eternal safety. In his willingness to endure the gravest danger—the agony of the cross—Jesus Christ accomplished the divine paradox. He took upon himself the danger of sin, death, and separation from God to ensure our eternal safety in the embrace of divine grace. He fought to ensure our safety, and our fight is to trust it is so.

The Righteousness We Need is Beyond Ourselves

Having spent a couple of years as a court and probation officer in the legal system, I've witnessed the ebb and flow of the courtroom's unique atmosphere. It's a place where emotions run high, stress and tension hang palpably in the air, and lives can change course with a single verdict. In this arena, one underlying theme consistently emerges: the relentless pursuit of justification.

Everyone present in the courtroom, from the accused to the accuser, from the lawyers to the judge, is entangled in this quest, driven either to justify themselves or to see justice served upon another. As I reflect on my experiences within those courtroom walls, I am reminded of the universal human yearning for justification, a longing that extends far beyond the legal system and permeates the very essence of our lives.

The world of the court is not an isolated realm but rather an example of the common human endeavor. It reflects our constant need to seek justification, both before God and our fellow human beings.

We strive to validate our existence, motives, actions, speech, decisions, relationships, and every aspect of our being. This relentless pursuit of justification is ingrained within us, shaping our happiness or unhappiness and is the standard human experience for us all.

In the words of Oswald Bayer, we catch a glimpse into his soul, which, in reality, mirrors the experience of every heart.

I constantly vacillate, even to the very end of life, between the judgment others make about me and my own judgment of myself. I am constantly trying to ascertain others' judgment about me and my own judgment of myself; I arrive at some point of calm and then become unsure of myself again. My identity is a floating one.

I resonate with this more than I want to admit. Thankfully, the solution to this ceaseless quest for justification lies in receiving a verdict of righteousness from the Sovereign God. We must let go—indeed, we must die—to every attempt at self-justification and passively accept it as an undeserved gift from beyond ourselves (Gal 2:15-16).

As Luther says, "God does not want to save us by our own but by an extraneous righteousness, one that does not originate in ourselves but comes to us from beyond ourselves, which does not arise on earth but comes from heaven."

You see, the gospel is news that declares us right with God, but to receive it, we must abandon our attempts at attaining our own righteousness (Gal 2:21). As we receive the gift of faith, and the old self's endeavors at self-justification are extinguished, we find peace and rest in Christ. God's justification of us leads to the precious gift of self-forgetfulness (2 Cor 5:14-15).

The passive righteousness of faith speaks to us, assuring us that we need not be preoccupied with ourselves. In this divine act, where God works decisively within us, we can live outside ourselves and wholly in him. Thus, we are shielded from self-judgment and liberated from the judgments of others, as these are no longer ultimate verdicts (1 Cor 4:3-5).

Until we embrace the death of our old selves and the birth of the new, our existence will be an incessant struggle for self-justification. We will exploit every available resource in the universe to validate our righteousness by any means possible. This self-centered pursuit is a prime manifestation of the sinful nature consuming our lives as we tirelessly strive for a righteousness we can never attain (Phil 3:1-11).

However, in Christ, our old selves are crushed, making way for the new self to breathe and flourish. As we find solace and affirmation in Christ for our existence and salvation, we are liberated from the wearisome task of self-justification—a task we could labor on indefinitely without success (Gal 3:17-21).

In Jesus, the matter is settled—we are justified—and therefore, we are free to channel our renewed energies into living out the principles of God's kingdom (Gal 5:1, 13)

A Cruciform Generosity: The God who Gives All

It is said that "money doesn't change people; it reveals them." Our resources serve as the tangible representation of our values and priorities, essentially composing our autobiography in objective and actionable terms. This idea aligns with the wisdom found in scripture, which suggests that money can serve as a litmus test for the condition of one's heart.

In the words of Jesus, "where your treasure is, there your heart will be also" (Matt 6:21). This holds true for both us and God. What God does with his wealth and resources is a window Into his heart, his values, his purposes.

Consider the expanse of God's resources. He declares, "every beast of the forest is mine, the cattle on a thousand hills" (Ps 50:10). King David acknowledges God's abundance, "Yours, Lord, is the greatness and the power and the glory and the majesty and the splendor, for everything in heaven and earth is yours. Yours, Lord, is the kingdom; you are exalted as head over all. Wealth and honor come from you; you are the ruler of all things."

As a self-sufficient God, he stands outside of us, dependent on no one and nothing. He is not "served by human hands, as though he needed anything, since he himself gives to all mankind life and breath and everything" (Acts 17:25). He is the resource, not the resourced.

Worship should naturally flow from grasping this, as Paul demonstrates: "Oh, the depth of the riches and wisdom and knowledge of God! How unsearchable are his judgments and how inscrutable his ways! 'For who has known the mind of the Lord, or who has been his counselor? Or who has given a gift to him that he might be repaid?' For from him and through him and to him are all things. To him be glory forever. Amen" (Rom 11:33-36).

Now, contemplate this God who owes nothing but gives everything. Paul writes, "for you know the grace of our Lord Jesus Christ, that though he was rich, yet for your sake he became poor, so that you through his poverty might become rich" (2 Cor 8:9).

The cross serves as an immovable flag planted in the soil of history, communicating to the world that our God is a God of boundless generosity. It is a symbol that unequivocally declares that the God of abundance is far from being stingy. He gives all, even himself.

What adds to the astonishment is that the wages we've earned for our sins and failures are death (Rom 3:23). God's redemptive generosity covers our debt, and, dear reader, our debt is great (Matt 18:21-35). As William Temple says, "All is of God; the only thing of my very own which I contribute to my redemption is the sin from which I need to be redeemed."

It's no surprise that eternity resounds with the voices of thousands proclaiming Jesus as worthy, as they declare, "for you were slain, and by your blood, you ransomed people for God from every tribe and language and people and nation" (Rev 5:9).

If resources reveal us, what does divine affluence show? Where does God's heart lie? What does he treasure and value most? Paul captures it beautifully when he describes Jesus as the one who "loved me and gave himself for me" (Gal 2:20; Eph 5:25). The cross, you see, is a testament to cherishing and forming us into "a people for his own possession" (1 Pet 2:9; Deut 7:6). The cross uncovers what God profoundly adores and what he chooses, and that is his people (Col 3:12).

The wealthy God impoverished for our sake is deeply humbling and liberating. The reality invokes worship and frees us to follow his footsteps with sacrificial generosity. In his letter to the Corinthians, Paul helps them understand the inseparable link between embracing the gospel of God and living a life of generosity. Having received

Christ as an indescribable gift, we are now called to walk in the freedom of the gospel and follow him as an example.

It's noteworthy that when Paul addresses the topic of giving, he doesn't point back to the Old Testament laws of tithes and offerings. Instead, he takes the believers on a journey down the Via Dolorosa, reminding them of the immeasurable generosity of God displayed through the gospel.

You see, the problem with tithing is that it only represents a portion of our resources. In the New Testament, there is no specific injunction that mandates tithing. However, what we do find is an infinitely wealthy God who willingly chose to impoverish himself in order to make us truly rich.

To truly follow Christ, he requires not just a portion of our lives but the entirety of who we are. Jesus said, "Whoever wants to be my disciple must deny themselves and take up their cross daily and follow me" (Lk 9:23). Ultimately, the generosity we are called to exhibit goes beyond a mere percentage. It encompasses our whole being, demonstrating the transformative power of the gospel in our lives.

As we grasp the depth of God's generosity in the cross, we are compelled to respond with a generosity that reflects his grace and love. When you know the answer is "nothing" to this most important question, everything changes: "What do you have that you have not received?" (1 Cor 4:7).

Take Yourself in Hand:
A Call for Rigorous Self-Talk

I have a playlist that runs through my head all day, it's my greatest hits—the things I say to myself over and over again. Some of those thoughts are helpful, many are not. Developing the discipline to interrupt these internal conversations proves crucial for mental and spiritual resilience. It might seem unusual, yet engaging in deliberate self-talk is an important biblical practice, providing the necessary remedy for replacing negative thought patterns.

In a systematic review of self-talk's impact, researcher David Tod concluded that the results "demonstrated positive effects of self-talk when it's positive, instructional, and motivational." In simpler terms, your internal dialogue has been scientifically proven to significantly influence your day-to-day performance as a human being.

Napoleon Hill may have overstated it, but he was still onto something when he said, "the single most influential force that controls your attitudes, beliefs, capabilities and emotions is repetition – the words you silently use, over and over again, in your internal dialogue with yourself."

From a biblical perspective, there is a call to take ourselves in hand, to do business with our souls through disciplined internal conversations. Note this example, "And David was greatly distressed, for the people spoke of stoning him, because all the people were bitter in soul, each for his sons and daughters. But David strengthened himself in the LORD his God" (1 Sam 30:6). The Psalms vividly demonstrate David's method of engaging with his soul to overcome internal discouragement. Here are a few more biblical instances highlighting the call to rigorous self-talk.

Command Your Soul to Gratitude. The Psalmist calls himself to worship: "Bless the LORD, O my soul, and all that is within me, bless his holy name! Bless the LORD, O my soul, and forget not all his benefits" (Ps 103:1-2). Twice, he directs his soul, urging it to recognize the goodness bestowed upon him by his Creator.

He proceeds to present all the evidence to his soul, illustrating why he should do so: "who forgives all your iniquity, who heals all your diseases who redeems your life from the pit, who crowns you with steadfast love and mercy, who satisfies you with good so that your youth is renewed like the eagle's" (Ps 103:3-5). The rest of the Psalm systematically provides reason after reason, illustrating that engaging with your soul involves offering motives to advance towards worship.

Call Your Soul out of Despair. When feeling low, the Psalmist refuses to lay down without a fight: "Why are you cast down, O my soul, and why are you in turmoil within me? Hope in God; for I shall again praise him, my salvation" (Ps 42:5). He asks himself tough questions, refusing to accept things as they are. Instead, he urges his soul to fight, to strive toward hope, envisioning a future beyond such a dark place.

Psalms 42-43 exemplify calling the soul out of a state of depression and towards hope. Notably, a similar sentiment is found in the self-talk of the woman who endured 12 years of bleeding: "For she said to herself, 'If I only touch his garment, I will be made well'" (Matt 9:21). Self-talk that helped push past doubt and led her to Jesus changed her entire life.

Speak Sense to Your Soul. The famous story of the prodigal son contains a critical piece of internal conversation. Having left home, severed family ties, and squandered his inheritance, he finds himself lost and starving. Out of this place we read: "But when he came to himself, he said, 'How many of my father's hired servants have more than enough bread, but I perish here with hunger! I will arise and go to my father, and I will say to him, 'Father, I have sinned against heaven and before you. I am no longer worthy to be called your son. Treat me as one of your hired servants'" (Lk 15:17-19).

That internal dialogue, undoubtedly prompted by God, drove him home. And as we know, the story's conclusion was remarkable. He reasoned with his soul, altering the trajectory of his future.

Demand Silence of Your Soul. Jesus' parables often contain compelling lessons in self-reflection. In a teaching about the perils of pursuing wealth, Jesus narrates a cautionary tale of impending danger for a man who squanders his riches, amassing an excess for the future. In the parable the man states: "And I will say to my soul, 'Soul, you have ample goods laid up for many years; relax, eat, drink, be merry'" (Matt 12:19).

His internal dialogue has dangerously led him astray. The parable unfolds further: "But God said to him, 'Fool! This night your soul is required of you, and the things you have prepared, whose will they be?' So is the one who lays up treasure for himself and is not rich toward God" (Matt 12:20-21). At times, the soul must be silenced, and the internal dialogue needs reproof and correction.

Preach the Gospel to Your Soul. Paul says that "faith comes from hearing, and hearing through the Word of Christ" (Rom 10:17). The gospel produces and sustains faith in our lives. That's why we sit under the preaching of God's Word, why we must remind each other of it, and also why we must regularly proclaim it to ourselves.

Gospel amnesia is a real thing—we often forget what God has done for us. Jerry Bridges states, "To preach the gospel to yourself, then, means that you continually face up to your own sinfulness and then flee to Jesus through faith in his shed blood and righteous life."

Put simply, we preach truth to our hearts, reminding ourselves of all that Christ is to us. Allowing the gospel to dominate our internal dialogue is where freedom resides, as truth alone has the power to set us free (Jn 8:32).

The One Unchanging and Unending Good

We are hard-wired to love beauty and goodness, instinctively recognizing their allure and being naturally drawn towards them. We may not be able to put it to words but we know it when we see it, we feel it when we experience it. C.S. Lewis suggests that while these encounters are impactful, they don't entirely satisfy our deeper longing; we crave more.

> *We do not want merely to see beauty, though, God knows, even that is bounty enough. We want something else which can hardly be put into words—to be united with the beauty we see, to pass into it, to receive it into ourselves, to bathe in it, to become part of it.*

Augustine, a theologian from 300 A.D., acknowledged this longing, asserting that without God, this yearning would remain unfulfilled: "You have made us for yourself, O Lord, and our hearts are restless until they find rest in you." In his influential book, "The City of God," Augustine asserts that the highest blessing and ultimate goodness lie in the unwavering certainty of uninterrupted communion with God.

His words resound with profound insight: "The beatitude desired by an intelligent being as its proper end will result only from the combination of an uninterrupted enjoyment of that immutable good which is God with deliverance from any doubt or deception concerning the eternity of its continuance." According to Augustine, God himself is the unchanging, unending, immutable good. The most privileged state a human being can attain is eternal union with this divine goodness and beauty

Augustine beautifully portrays this gift in two ways. First, it involves an incessant and undisturbed enjoyment of God, a perpetual communion with our Maker. Second, it encompasses an unwavering certainty that this fellowship with God will endure for eternity, never to be interrupted or severed. At the heart of enjoyment lies the profound reality of an eternal and secure communion with the Triune God.

Within his discussion on the immutable good, Augustine draws an intriguing contrast between the fallen angels and the people of God. The fallen angels knew the intimacy of fellowship with God but lacked the assurance of everlasting communion with him. Conversely, the people of God are promised both aspects of goodness. Our highest state of joy includes the certainty of never losing connection to the immutable good.

This profound grace emphasizes the marvel of the gospel— despite our shared sin with angels, God chose to rescue us. The author of Hebrews tells us that the Son of God chose to take on "flesh and blood" partake of the "same things" as us in order to destroy sin, death and the devil (Heb 2:14-15).

He then proceeds to say, "For surely it is not angels that he helps, but he helps the offspring of Abraham. Therefore, he had to be made like his brothers in every respect, so that he might become a merciful and faithful high priest in the service of God, to make propitiation for the sins of the people" (Heb 2:16-17).

Salvation is not available for fallen angels; he does not provide them saving help. Yet, we have sinned just like them, rebelled just like them, and failed God just like them. In his overwhelming mercy he chooses to rescue us, hence the need for him to become like us in every way in order to provide the perfect sacrifice in our place. Our experience of the immutable good---of fellowship with God for eternity is pure gift that comes at a tremendous cost to God. This is good news for us.

Salvation isn't extended to fallen angels; saving help isn't provided for them. However, we've sinned like them, rebelled similarly, and disappointed God just as they did. Yet, in overwhelming mercy, God chooses to rescue us.

Hence, the necessity for him to fully embody our nature, offering the perfect sacrifice in our stead. Our possession of unchanging goodness—eternal fellowship with God—is a pure gift, one that comes at an immense cost to God. This indeed is wonderful news for us.

In John 17:3, Jesus himself prays, "And this is eternal life, that they know you, the only true God, and Jesus Christ whom you have sent." Here, Jesus articulates that eternal life is intimately tied to knowing God and experiencing an unbroken fellowship with him. This is the gift emanating from his death and resurrection: a life characterized by the ongoing delight in God's presence and the certainty of an everlasting relationship.

The highest state of human flourishing is found in an uninterrupted enjoyment of God, coupled with the unwavering assurance of an eternal and unbroken fellowship with him. This dual aspect of assurance distinguishes the experience of the people of God from the fallen angels.

Scripture further affirms this truth, emphasizing that eternal life and true joy are discovered in the continual presence and communion with the Triune God. There is a deep longing within the human heart for true goodness and beauty. Augustine reminds us that this is can only be found in a never-ending and secure union with the immutable good, which is God himself.

8

Hallowed Be Thy Gains: Getting After Spiritual Fitness

The "hallowed be thy gains" gym meme, one of my favorites, features praying hands holding weights and humorously ties dedication to physical gains with a spiritual fitness twist. Studies indicate that exercising with a partner or in a group significantly boosts workout results due to mutual accountability and motivation.

Similarly, in the realm of spiritual well-being, having a supportive community fosters growth, encouragement, and a deeper connection to one's faith. Both physical and spiritual gains accrue from the power of companionship and shared goals.

Paul encourages us to pursue such gains; he understands the importance of spiritual and physical synergy, as well as the need for community. In his letter to the Corinthians, he models the pursuit of godly gains:

> *Do you not know that in a race all the runners run, but only one receives the prize? So run that you may obtain it. Every athlete exercises self-control in all things. They do it to receive a perishable wreath, but we an imperishable. So I do not run aimlessly; I do not box as one beating the air. But I discipline my body and keep it under control, lest after preaching to others I myself should be disqualified (1 Cor 9:24-27).*

Exercise, running, fighting—all demand discipline and self-control to attain the prize. This passage notably describes the convergence of physical and spiritual discipline. The link between spiritual and physical fitness is clear and mutually influential.

In another context, Paul provides a similar emphasis on their value while prioritizing one over the other: "While bodily training holds some value, godliness holds value in every way, promising benefits for the present and the afterlife" (1 Tim 4:8).

We are unmistakably called to "get after it." However, we can't do it alone—we need gym buddies. The book of Hebrews sheds light on this need: "But exhort one another every day, as long as it is called 'today,' that none of you may be hardened by the deceitfulness of sin. For we have come to share in Christ, if indeed we hold our original confidence firm to the end. As it is said, 'Today, if you hear his voice, do not harden your hearts as in the rebellion'" (Heb 3:13-15).

This passage emphasizes the urgency of daily interaction with other like-minded followers. The author emphasizes that we must not focus on what transpired yesterday or what awaits us tomorrow, but on the present moment—the "today." It is in this very moment that we need to engage in encouragement, and support for one another. This passage calls for spiritual fitness, emphasizing the resilience hammered out through the help of others.

The deceitfulness of sin poses a constant threat to our faith. It seeks to harden our hearts and draw us away from God. Thus, we are called to support each other, taking a continuous and active role in addressing the corrosive effects of sin in our lives.

The strategy for this daily engagement is found in encouragement. When we come alongside one another, lifting each other up with gospel admonition and support, we counteract the deceitfulness of sin and foster a community of perseverance and grit.

The community of faith becomes a bulwark against the downward pull of sin, constantly interrupting its corrupting influence in our lives. In other words, together we combat the things that threaten our spiritual gains.

Our lives depend on daily bread for sustenance, but our perseverance in faith depends on daily encouragement. Each new day presents an opportunity to give and receive the gospel-centered hope we need to navigate life's challenges and remain steadfast in our faith in Christ. If you're chasing those spiritual gains, get a workout buddy and get in front of the gospel.

Wage war against your sin and strive to live authentically before the face of God. Embrace struggle knowing that it is the primary context where God works out endurance and character in us (Rom 5:3-5). And finally, don't quit, ever. As Winston Churchill urged: "This is the lesson: never give in, never give in, never, never, never, never-in nothing, great or small, large or petty—never give in except to convictions of honor and good sense."

Taking the Golden Rule to Heart, and Everywhere Else

Some years back, a close family friend experienced the loss of her mother after a long battle with dementia. Witnessing her journey, marked by grace, patience, and transparency, left a lasting impression on me. She navigated the difficult decisions, the twists and turns of grief, pain, and even joy with remarkable strength.

During a conversation, she shared a simple yet profound insight that shaped her perspective throughout the journey: "I put myself in her shoes and asked, 'How would I want someone to treat me?'"

This approach, rooted in the golden rule, guided her decisions, both significant and seemingly insignificant. Her conversations with her mother, the time spent together, choices regarding living situations, and the selection of caregivers were all informed by her genuine desire to treat her mother as she would want to be treated.

Reflecting on this conversation, I realized the depth and significance of the commandment known as the golden rule. Its simplicity belies its profound truth, particularly when applied to caring for a loved one with dementia. Furthermore, I recognized that I had not fully explored the far-reaching implications of this commandment given by Christ. While I had touched the surface, I had not grasped its transformative power. Let's examine the text together.

In Matthew's account, we find the following: "So whatever you wish that others would do to you, do also to them, for this is the Law and the Prophets" (Matt 7:12). On this command hangs the entirety of the law and the prophets. Its significance cannot be overstated. The moral principles encapsulated in the Old Testament teachings find their essence in this commandment.

Jesus himself used similar language when discussing the interconnected concept of loving one's neighbor as oneself (Matt 22:39-40). In other words, this commandment is intended to permeate every aspect of our lives. It should illuminate every corner, guiding all our relationships.

It is notable that Jesus' words in this passage go beyond being a mere maxim, a wise suggestion, or a helpful guideline. He is conveying to his followers that this command is not optional; it is at the core of our relational posture. It calls us to transcend self-centeredness and focus on others, transferring our concerns and care onto them.

We are called to love and serve our neighbors with the same passion and dedication that we have for ourselves. Jesus stands as the ultimate embodiment of selfless love for the neighbor. Paul echoes this call in his exhortation for believers to accept and serve one another based on Christ's example: "For even Christ did not please himself but, as it is written: 'The insults of those who insult you have fallen on me'" (Rom 15:3).

Jesus lived a life dedicated to serving and pleasing his neighbors, even to the point of sacrificing himself on the cross. Through his death and resurrection, he secured our salvation and exemplified the highest standard of love for our neighbors. He remains our ultimate gift and substitute before he becomes our example. Jesus alone fulfilled the greatest commandments and the golden imperative perfectly, serving his neighbors as they ought to be served. He is our Savior, our source of righteousness as we trust in him.

Through our union with Jesus, the Father sees us as having perfectly obeyed the golden rule. By virtue of our new nature and the indwelling of the Holy Spirit, we are empowered to grow in obedience to him as we engage with our neighbors. We can be grateful for the transformative power of the gospel, which justifies us, sets us free, and enables us to undergo a process of continual change.

This connection between gospel freedom and neighborly love is further illuminated in Paul's words: We see the connection of gospel freedom and neighborly love in Paul's words, "You, my brothers and sisters, were called to be free. But do not use your freedom to indulge the flesh; rather, serve one another humbly in love" (Gal 5:13).

How does this translate into everyday life? The first step in applying the golden rule is to contemplate how we desire to be treated in various situations. When we are fearful, we yearn for reassurance. In times of pain, we crave compassion. In moments of anger, we hope for patience. When we experience joy, we want others to share in our delight. In times of failure, we long for grace and understanding.

The second step is to consider the different relational contexts in which we find ourselves. How can we apply this commandment in our homes, workplaces, communities, and places of worship? Each context presents unique relational dynamics. If we were to intentionally apply the golden rule in every interaction, our relationships would be transformed. People would feel seen, heard, and valued. Our actions would demonstrate genuine care and empathy.

How different would things be if this truth guided our engagement in every relationship? How would it impact others and ourselves? Embracing the golden rule requires intentionality and sacrifice. It calls us to emulate the character of Christ, who exemplified selflessness and prioritized the well-being of others. He embodied the command to love our neighbors and exemplified the essence of the golden imperative.

As with every commandment, we must revisit and anchor ourselves in the good news. The gospel that justifies us, sets us free, and transforms us, is the gospel that enables us to live out this golden rule in our daily lives. May we strive to integrate the golden rule into the fabric of our lives, extending kindness, empathy, and love to all those we encounter.

The Power of the Personal Pronoun

When my daughter was two years old, she brightened my day every time I returned home after a long day of work. Without fail, her arrival was marked by her tiny frame springing toward me, grabbing my legs, and screaming with delight, "Daddy, Daddy, Daddy, my Daddy!" She would repeatedly say, "my daddy is home."

My daughter taught me the precious nature of the personal pronoun. "Daddy" is wonderful, but "my Daddy" is even more profound. It conveys belonging, intimacy, and the uniqueness of our relationship. She was expressing that among all the dads out there, I am the one who belongs to her. All encapsulated within the simple word "my."

It is believed that Martin Luther once said, "The Christian faith is a matter of personal pronouns." The richest personal pronouns in Scripture denote a dual ownership between God and his people. We belong to God, and God belongs to us. We are his people, and he is our God. God's people are his inheritance, and God is the inheritance of his people (Ps 95:6-7).

Luther emphasized, "Read with great emphasis these words, 'me,' 'for me,' and accustom yourself to accept and apply to yourself this 'me' with unwavering faith. The words OUR, US, FOR US, should be inscribed in golden letters — the person who does not believe in them is not a Christian."

Luther also underscored the importance of connecting the personal pronoun to the redemptive work of Jesus: "Note especially the pronoun 'our' and its significance. You will readily acknowledge that Christ gave himself for the sins of Peter, Paul, and others who were worthy of such grace. But in moments of doubt, it becomes challenging to believe that Christ gave himself for your sins. Our emotions shy away from personally applying the pronoun 'our,' and we hesitate to engage with God until we feel worthy through good deeds."

Every time I step through the door, my daughter teaches me an invaluable lesson about God. He is "my Father." Through the labor of his Son, he delights in hearing that designation from my lips — and that's astonishing.

The joy I experience daily is a small fragment of God's joy over the people he calls his own. This is a mutual delight, a reciprocal joy. God delights in calling us his people, and we are overjoyed to call him our God. All this because Jesus took our sins upon himself. Remember the power of the personal pronoun, friends.

Know Your Enemy: A Short Theology of the Devil

If you are in a fight, knowing your enemy is paramount, a principle highlighted by Sun Tzu in the Art of War: "If you know the enemy and you know yourself, you need not fear the result of a hundred battles. If you know yourself but not the enemy, for every victory gained you will also suffer a defeat." The devil is one such enemy.

Where did the devil come from, and what does Scripture reveal about him? It's an important topic that can significantly shape our understanding of this powerful adversary. Let's look at the origin, nature, and ultimate fate of the devil.

First and foremost, the term "devil" derives from the Greek word "diabolos," meaning "slanderer." The devil is also referred to as Satan, which means "accuser," as well as by other names such as Lucifer, the serpent, the dragon, the tempter, and Beelzebub. According to Scripture, the devil was initially an angel created by God. Like all angels, he was designed to worship and obey God.

It is believed that the devil held a position of leadership among the angelic beings, much like the archangels Michael and Gabriel. However, it's crucial to emphasize that the devil is in no way equal to God. He lacks divine power, cannot be present in multiple places simultaneously, and is entirely dependent on God for his initial and continued existence (Dan 8:15-26, 9:21-27, 10:13-21, 12:1; Jude 1:9; Rev 12:1-12; Lk 1:19-38).

Secondly, the devil's fall from grace is attributed to his succumbing to pride. Scripture suggests that he rebelled against God, harboring a desire to seize his throne and establish his own dominion. This rebellion instigated a war in heaven, resulting in the devil and his followers being cast out. The book of Revelation vividly portrays this cosmic battle, depicting the dragon (symbolizing the devil) and his angels being defeated and thrown down to the earth (Rev 12:1-9).

Other passages in the Bible, such as Ezekiel 28:1-26 and Isaiah 14:12-15, provide further insight into the pride and rebellion that led to the devil's downfall. The Bible also reveals that these fallen angels, known as demons or unclean spirits, actively engage in attacking, tempting, and seeking to destroy human beings on Earth (Rev 12:9; Jn 10:10). Numerous references to demons can be found throughout the New Testament, highlighting their malevolent presence and influence (Matt 8:16, 12:43; Mk 1:34; Lk 4:41; Acts 5:16, 8:7).

Thirdly, the devil's pivotal role in human history can be traced back to the Garden of Eden. In the form of a serpent, he approached Adam and Eve and enticed them to disobey God, introducing sin and its consequences into the world (Gen 3). Yet, even in this dark moment, God proclaimed his plan of redemption. He pronounced that the offspring of the woman would crush the head of the serpent, signifying the ultimate victory over evil (Gen 3:15).

The entire narrative of the Bible centers around God's unfolding plan to dismantle the work of the devil and rescue humanity from the grip of sin. This divine rescue mission finds its fulfillment in Jesus Christ. Through his sacrificial death on the cross and triumphant resurrection, Jesus dealt a decisive blow to the powers of darkness, including the devil himself (1 Jn 3:8; Col 2:15; Heb 2:14-18).

Fourthly, the Bible provides guidance on how to navigate the spiritual warfare in which we find ourselves. It teaches us to submit to God, recognizing that he holds the ultimate power over the enemy. When we humbly yield to God and put our trust in him, the devil is forced to flee from us (Jas 4:7). The victory over the enemy has been won by Jesus Christ, and when we place our faith in him, we are protected by his triumph.

Throughout the New Testament, we witness the authority and power of Jesus over demons, as they are cast out and driven away in his presence and by the invocation of his name (Mk 5:1-20; Acts 16:16-18). Regardless of the names or lengths of their existence, demons tremble in the presence of God (Jas 2:19) and are terrified by the authority of Jesus (Matt 8:28-30). Thus, as believers, our response to the darkness and spiritual attacks is to walk in the light of Christ, relying on his power and truth to overcome (Eph 5:8; 1 Jn 1:7).

Fifthly, the Bible explicitly recognizes that we are in the midst of a spiritual war. The devil continues to launch attacks, temptations, and deceitful schemes in an attempt to lead us astray. However, Scripture encourages us to put on the full armor of God, equipping ourselves for the battle against the spiritual forces of evil. This armor includes elements such as truth, righteousness, faith, salvation, the Word of God, and prayer (Eph 6:10-18). Each component of the armor represents an essential aspect of our spiritual preparation, enabling us to stand firm and resist the devil's schemes.

Finally, the ultimate destiny of the devil and his demons is sealed by God's judgment. The book of Revelation reveals that, at the return of Jesus Christ, the devil and all his demonic forces will be cast into the lake of fire, experiencing everlasting punishment and separation from God (2 Pet 2:4; Reve 20:1-3). We've observed that Scripture serves as a battle guide, unveiling the enemy's origin, nature, purposes, and destiny. Above all, analyzing into adversary's work leads us to the supreme warrior who fights on our behalf and ultimately triumphs by crushing the serpent's head beneath our feet (Rom 16:20).

Learning to Keep to the Present

"Remember today is the tomorrow you worried about yesterday," as Dale Carnegie cleverly remarked. If like me, you feel that the past and future tend to steal from the present, you're not alone. To help us anchor in the moment, we'll turn to guidance from Blaise Pascal, a distinguished 17th century figure celebrated for his work in Christian philosophy, science, and mathematics.

Pascal's profound insights, found in his notable work "Pensées," which means "thoughts" in French, cover a wide range of topics, offering valuable perspectives. Among them, Pascal's reflections on living in the present are particularly thought-provoking and provide us with a challenge. His quote, though lengthy, is worth reading in full:

> *We never keep to the present. We recall the past; we anticipate the future as if we found it too slow in coming and were trying to hurry it up, or we recall the past as if to stay its too rapid flight. We are so unwise that we wander about in times that do not belong to us, and do not think of the only one that does; so vain that we dream of time that are not and blindly flee the only one that is. The fact is that the present usually hurts. We thrust it out of sight because it distresses us, and if we find it enjoyable, we are sorry to see it slip away. We try to give it the support of the future, and think how we are going to arrange things over which we have no control for a time we can never be sure of reaching. Let each of us examine his thoughts; he will find them wholly concerned with the past or the future. We almost never*

think of the present, and if we do think of it, it is only to see
what light it throws on our plans for the future. The present is
never our end. The past and the present are our means, the
future alone our end. Thus, we never actually live, but hope to
live, and since we always planning how to be happy, it is
inevitable that we should never be so.

Pascal astutely observes our tendency to dwell in the past or eagerly anticipate the future, as if dissatisfied with the pace of the present and seeking to hasten its passing. We often find ourselves wandering through moments that do not belong to us, neglecting the one that truly matters—the present. We become so preoccupied with time that does not exist, blindingly fleeing from the only time that does.

The reason behind our inclination to evade the present lies in the discomfort it often brings. This is a sobering reality. When confronted with the present, we tend to push it aside because it hurts. And when we do find joy in the present, we sorrowfully watch it slip away. Instead of embracing the present for what it is, we attempt to seek support from an uncertain future. We obsessively ponder over matters beyond our control, planning for a time we may never reach.

Pascal reveals a sobering reality: we often neglect to truly live in the present. The past and the present become mere tools, means to an end, while the future alone becomes our ultimate goal. Consequently, we find ourselves trapped in an endless cycle of hoping to live rather than experiencing genuine life. We continually strive for happiness, perpetually planning for the future, and inadvertently rob ourselves of the fullness of the present moment.

Expanding on Pascal's wisdom, we recognize that living in the present requires a shift in perspective. It demands a conscious effort to let go of past regrets and future anxieties, and to fully embrace the here and now. It summons the courage to face the pain the moment can bring and the unanticipated joy that may also await us. It invites us to appreciate the beauty, challenges, and opportunities that each present moment brings. By immersing ourselves in the present, we can cultivate a deeper sense of gratitude, contentment, and awareness.

Scripture offers guidance and encouragement in this pursuit of living fully in the present. In Matthew 6:34, Jesus teaches, "Therefore do not be anxious about tomorrow, for tomorrow will be anxious for itself. Sufficient for the day is its own trouble." This reminds us to focus on the present day and trust God's provision for each moment.

Similarly, Paul encourages believers in Philippians 4:6-7, saying, "Do not be anxious about anything, but in everything by prayer and supplication with thanksgiving let your requests be made known to God. And the peace of God, which surpasses all understanding, will guard your hearts and your minds in Christ Jesus." These passages remind us of the importance of surrendering our worries and fears to God, finding peace in the present moment.

Blaise Pascal's reflections point to the significance of embracing the present. Rather than being consumed by the past or fixated on the future, we are called to fully live in the moment. Just as we need God's provision of daily bread, we need his support in embracing the moments of the day. We know this is easier said than done, but it is a fight worth fighting.

Our Infinite Capacity for
Taking Things for Granted

Dr. Robert Emmons, a Psychology professor at the University of California, Davis, has devoted his entire professional career to researching gratitude. He encapsulates his research findings in this field as follows:

> *In the past few years, there has been a tremendous increase in the accumulation of scientific evidence showing the contribution of gratitude to psychological and social well-being. Clinical trials indicate that the practice of gratitude can have dramatic and lasting positive effects in a person's life. It can lower blood pressure, improve immune function, promote happiness and well-being, and spur acts of helpfulness, generosity, and cooperation. Additionally, gratitude reduces lifetime risk for depression, anxiety, and substance abuse disorders.*

Imagine then how ingratitude impacts us. The difficulty lies in the fact that ingratitude is my default stance. Entitlement and thanklessness are deeply rooted, destructive attitudes that have plagued us throughout history.

Like an aggressive cancer, they consume and destroy, robbing life of joy and wonder. These mindsets restrict and narrow the abundant gift of life, reducing it to a self-centered transaction where personal benefit takes precedence. They blind us to the true nature of life as a gift, causing us to overlook its inherent worth and focusing solely on personal gain.

At the core of this destructive way of being is a self-centered posture that demands the world to revolve around "me." When expectations go unmet and the universe fails to comply, internal and external turmoil ensues. As Martin Luther declared, this sickness originated from the fall when humanity "curved inward," becoming preoccupied with self.

Since then, as Aldous Huxley astutely observed, "most human beings have an almost infinite capacity for taking things for granted. Though it stings, the only appropriate response, as the Latin phrase goes, is "Mea Culpa"—acknowledging, "I am at fault."

Psalm 100 serves as a corrective to ingratitude, a guide for cultivating a posture of gratitude. It emphasizes the connection between joy and thanksgiving, and grounds this thanksgiving in two fundamental aspects: creation and covenant. Understanding and embracing these truths can transform our perspective on life and lead us to a deeper sense of gratitude.

The psalm begins with a call to celebration and praise, highlighting the link between joy and thanksgiving: "Make a joyful noise to the Lord, all the earth! Serve the Lord with gladness" (Ps 100:1). As Karl Barth eloquently stated, joy is the "simplest form of gratitude." When we experience joy, it naturally flows into expressions of thankfulness. It is a response to recognizing and appreciating the gifts we have received.

This joyful gratitude is rooted in a knowledge of God. The psalm declares, "Know that the Lord, he is God! It is he who made us, not we ourselves. We are his people, and the sheep of his pasture" (Ps 100:2). This verse reminds us that God is the Creator, and we are his created beings. It is important to be reminded that we did not bring ourselves into existence; rather, our very existence is a gift from God.

As creatures, we are fundamentally dependent on God. Our existence, every breath we take, and all that we have are gifts from him. This understanding forms the foundation of gratitude. If we recognize that our very being is a gift, then it follows that everything that comes our way is also a gift.

Life itself is a precious gift from God. As Paul writes, "What do you have that you did not receive?" (1 Cor 4:7). This perspective shifts our focus from entitlement to gratitude, allowing us to embrace life as a continual outpouring of God's goodness.

G.K. Chesterton once remarked that "All goods look better when they look like gifts." When we view life through the lens of gratitude, we begin to see everything as a gift from God. This perspective transforms our perception of the world around us and deepens our appreciation for the provisions we often take for granted.

The psalm concludes with a powerful reason for giving thanks: "For the Lord is good; his steadfast love endures forever, and his faithfulness to all generations" (Ps 100:5). This grounds our thanksgiving in the goodness, steadfast love, and faithfulness of God. The language of steadfast love is closely tied to the concept of covenant—a bond of loyalty, faithfulness, and unfailing commitment. It is a love that is unchanging, rooted in promises and sealed by blood.

God's covenant promises are made by a God who is trustworthy and never fails to fulfill his word. The ultimate expression of his love and faithfulness is seen in the sending of his Son, Jesus Christ, to fulfill his promises to us and provide redemption and hope. Understanding the wonder and certainty of these blood-bought promises fills our hearts with gratitude.

In a world that constantly tugs us toward self-centeredness and discontentment, these truths serve as a powerful reminder of the profound influence gratitude can wield in our lives. They encourage us to pivot our attention from entitlement to appreciation and from ingratitude to thankfulness.

As we integrate gratitude into our everyday lives and heed the call of Psalm 100, recognizing that each breath we take, every provision we receive, and every promise of God is a cherished gift, we open ourselves to the divine abundance that surround us. This shift in perspective leads to genuine human flourishing.

The Forsaken Places are Where He Chooses to Go

Martin Luther, a key figure in the Protestant Reformation, profoundly understood the significance of the cross of Christ. He recognized that the cross was not merely a saving event but the very heart of theology and God's self-revelation.

Luther's understanding of the cross went beyond its role in salvation; he believed it to be the definitive act that revealed God's nature and character. In his words, "the cross of Christ is the only instruction in the Word of God there is, the purest theology."

The cross of Calvary was a game changer, forever marking the Triune God as the "God of the cross." Robert Kolb aptly states, "the cross is where human beings can see what God's experience, God's disposition—even God's essence— really are." If we would find God, Kolb says we must look in the most unexpected places. We find him as a "child in a crib, as a criminal on a cross, and as a corpse in a crypt." In other words, he is found in the forsaken places.

Luther derived these assertions from his careful study of Paul's writings, particularly his letters to the Corinthians. In 1 Corinthians 1-2, Paul argues that the cross shatters our preconceived notions of wisdom, power, and glory, introducing a radical redefinition of reality. The cross turns the world upside down, challenging our human understanding and revealing God's wisdom in what the world considers foolishness, God's power in what the world perceives as weakness, and God's glory in the midst of humility.

When the cross becomes the center of our lives, when we orbit around the Crucified God, everything changes. We begin to view the world through a different lens, one shaped by the transformative power of the cross. Our decisions may seem counterintuitive to others, guided by a wisdom that surpasses human understanding.

We start to value things that society may despise—mercy over judgment, sacrificial love over self-centeredness, and humility over pride. In this new perspective, we discern the presence of God in unexpected places, recognizing his hand at work in the marginalized, the broken, and the least among us.

The key takeaway here is crucial. The cross, despite its profound sense of forsakenness, is precisely where God's overwhelming presence shines through. Many times, we may feel abandoned, convinced that God has left us, especially in the depths of addiction, a heart-wrenching divorce, debilitating depression, an estranged relationship, or the loss of a family pillar.

But this is precisely what the cross conveys – God can be found right in those chaotic, forsaken places. It's in the very spots where others hesitate to tread and where you're hesitant to discuss, that God reveals himself.

As we contemplate the profound truths expressed by Martin Luther and Paul, we are invited to center our lives on the cross of Christ. It is through the cross that we find redemption, but it is also through the cross that we gain a new perspective, a transformed way of living, and a deeper understanding of the heart of God. Press in to the cross, friends, you will find him there.

Faith and Grit: How the Gospel Creates Strength

"You then, my child, be strengthened by the grace that is in Christ Jesus" (2 Tim 2:1). In this passage, Paul provides valuable insight into the link between strength and the gospel. He emphasizes that the source of strength for the Christian journey is none other than God's grace. Paul's words affirm the foundational principle that salvation and growth in the Christian life are rooted in God's unmerited favor, which is expressed through the gospel.

The journey of a Christian begins and continues by grace alone. As Paul asserts in other places, we are saved by grace (Eph 2:8-10), but here he shows us we are also strengthened by it. This highlights the ongoing significance of grace in every aspect of the believer's life. Grace is not merely a one-time event but a continuous supply of divine power that sustains and empowers us.

Paul further clarifies that the essence of this grace is found in Christ Jesus. Here, he points us toward a gospel-centered understanding of strength. The grace of God is fully embodied in the person and work of Jesus Christ—his incarnation, crucifixion, resurrection, and exaltation. As we immerse ourselves in the gospel message, meditating on it, studying it, and making it a part of our lives, we experience the strengthening power of God's grace.

The Greek word translated as "be strengthened" conveys the idea of becoming strong or empowered. It is in the present passive imperative form, indicating that strength is an ongoing process and command for believers. While we are called to pursue strength, we must recognize that it is ultimately a gift from God. Just as a sailor must position their sails to catch the wind, we are called to position ourselves in a way that allows the winds of the gospel to push us forward and strengthen us continually.

In light of this, proximity to the gospel becomes crucial in determining both strength and weakness in the Christian journey. Drawing an analogy to a cell phone's battery, Paul highlights that full strength reflects recent close proximity to its power source, while weakness indicates distance from it.

Similarly, our spiritual strength waxes and wanes depending on our nearness to the gospel. When we distance ourselves from the gospel, we can expect to experience weakness. Conversely, when we intentionally place ourselves in situations where we encounter and engage with the gospel regularly, we will be strengthened.

In essence, Paul urges us to recognize that weakness is not a mystery in the Christian life but a direct consequence of our proximity to or distance from the gospel. Embracing and embodying the gospel message in our lives leads to a continuous flow of divine strength that equips us for every challenge and empowers us to live faithfully and boldly for Christ (Phil 4:13).

Forced to Rest: God's Commands as Necessary Gifts

The best bosses are the ones that make you go home on time. They don't crack the whip; instead, they gently pull back on the reins. They don't model burnout; they exemplify work-life balance. They understand that innovation, productivity, and quality work are closely linked to a well-rested workforce.

According to one study, America ranks as the fourth most fatigued nation in the world, a fact we know intuitively about ourselves. At times, being compelled to stop can be the most valuable gift, especially when we consider our fatigue levels — the gift of being directed to leave work, take some time off, set aside work demands, and embrace the Sabbath.

In the Gospel of Mark, the theme of Sabbath arises repeatedly, often accompanied by controversy. The religious teachers scrutinize Jesus, seeking to find fault with his understanding and observance of the Sabbath. In one instance, Jesus offers a profound insight on the purpose of the Sabbath: "Then Jesus said to them, 'The Sabbath was made to meet the needs of people, and not people to meet the requirements of the Sabbath.' So, the Son of Man is Lord, even over the Sabbath!" (Mk 2:27-28).

In this statement, Jesus unveils the true intention behind God's establishment of the Sabbath. It was not a rigid set of rules to burden people, but rather a provision to be enjoyed. The Sabbath was created to meet a fundamental human need—the need for rest, rejuvenation, and communion with God. It is both a gift and an imperative, a gracious invitation to partake in God's rest. In essence, Jesus emphasizes that the

Sabbath was made for the well-being of humanity, highlighting the priority of human need over strict adherence to rules.

This understanding aligns with a reading of the creation account in Genesis 1-2, where the seventh day is portrayed as an open-ended invitation to enter into God's rest. The Sabbath is not a mere legalistic obligation; rather, it is an invitation to experience the fullness of God's provision and presence.

Viewing one of the Ten Commandments, specifically the commandment regarding the Sabbath, in this light prompts us to question whether the other commandments also carry the same purpose—to meet the needs of humanity.

Indeed, when we examine the Ten Commandments as a whole, we can discern a pattern of God's gracious provision for human flourishing. Each commandment serves as a guide for a life of wholeness and harmony. For example, honoring one's parents fosters healthy relationships and social stability.

Respecting the sanctity of life ensures the preservation of human dignity. Practicing honesty and integrity promotes trust and community. The commandments are not burdens imposed upon people; they are gifts given to enhance human flourishing and facilitate a deeper relationship with God and one another.

The words of Jesus in Mark's gospel challenge us to reframe our understanding of the commandments. They invite us to recognize that God's laws are not meant to be oppressive burdens but rather divine provisions for our well-being.

As we reflect on the nature of the commandments as gifts, we are reminded of Psalm 119:97-98: "Oh, how I love your law! I meditate on it all day long. Your commands are always with me and make me wiser than my enemies." These verses express the psalmist's delight in God's law and the wisdom it imparts. The commandments are not restrictions, but rather sources of wisdom and guidance that lead to a flourishing life.

May we approach the commandments with a renewed perspective, seeing them as gifts that meet our deepest needs and enable us to live in alignment with God's intentions. Let us embrace the restorative power of the Sabbath and the transformative wisdom embedded within the commandments, knowing that they are expressions of God's love and provision for our lives.

Sacred Uprising: The Cross as God's Powerful Protest

The cross is not only the instrument of our rescue, it's the lens through which we must view all things. For example, wisdom, strength, and authority are redefined by that dark moment outside Jerusalem two thousand years ago (1 Cor 1:18-31).

The Ten Commandments must also be reworked through this prism. The third commandment calls on us to refrain from using God's name in vain (Ex 20:7). How might the crucifixion inform how we would understand this imperative?

The cross, according to Jurgen Moltmann, represents "God's protest against the misuse of his name." Throughout history, humanity has often conceived various images of God and attached his name to ideas and causes that fundamentally contradict his true nature.

Regrettably, some of the most abhorrent acts in human history have been justified and carried out in the name of God. However, the cross stands as an enduring symbol, steadfastly revolting against any abuse or misuse of God's name.

The cross, with its humble and sacrificial service, becomes the defining expression of God's character for us. It reveals a God who is willing to give himself selflessly for the sake of humanity. In the face of manipulation and distortion, the cross unveils the true essence of God's nature—love, compassion, justice, and mercy.

Martin Luther, the Protestant Reformer, stated, "while we are forbidden from misusing his name, we are also commanded to use it in the service of what is true and good." When actions are carried out in the name of God without the foundational principle of the cross, they are exposed as impostors, misrepresenting his true identity.

The cross becomes the litmus test, separating genuine devotion from misguided fanaticism. It challenges us to scrutinize our own beliefs and actions, ensuring that they align with the self-giving love demonstrated on the cross.

To truly comprehend the nature of God, we must embrace the significance of the cross of Christ. It is through the lens of the cross that we gain a deeper understanding of God's heart and character. The cross compels us to reject any form of violence, oppression, or hatred that masquerades as acts done in the name of God.

It warns us of the dire consequences of misusing God's name, as G.K. Chesterton says, "no man can break any of the Ten Commandments. He can only break himself against them." Ultimately, the cross invites us to embody the humble love displayed by Jesus, extending it to all humanity.

By embracing the cross as God's protest against the misuse of his name, we not only honor his true identity but also commit ourselves to live lives characterized by love, justice, and service. The cross challenges us to be discerning, critically examining any claims made in the name of God to ensure they align with the transformative message of the cross.

In essence, the cross is a powerful symbol that safeguards the integrity of God's name and defines his character for us. It urges us to be vigilant against any distortion or abuse of his name, reminding us that true understanding of God can only be attained through the lens of the cross—the ultimate manifestation of divine love and redemption.

18

Living, Active, and Sharp:
The Penetrating Word of God

Ups and downs, valleys and mountains, hope and despair—these are the contours of the path for those attempting to walk with God. Life is tough, and so is following Jesus, which is expected if we have closely tracked what he has promised (Jn 16:33; Phil 1:29). Yet, in the pain cave and the valley of despair, God's Word penetrates the darkness and agony.

I have found that God's Word is consistently timely—whether it's the bitter cry of Job as he argues with God about his pain, the heartfelt laments of the Psalmists, the stern but necessary rebukes found in the book of Hebrews, the soothing promises of Paul, the winsome guidance of Proverbs, or the stories of Jesus kneeling to look a broken human in the face—they all bring life when and where we need it most.

There are resources in God's Word waiting for you, when life hits you in ways you didn't see coming, the Word of God stands ready with exactly what you need. Consider the penetrating nature of Scripture: "For the Word of God is living and active, sharper than any two-edged sword, piercing to the division of soul and of spirit, of joints and of marrow, and discerning the thoughts and intentions of the heart." (Heb 4:12).

Living, active, and sharp, it is in the business of piercing, discerning, and providing exactly what we need, precisely when we need it. This is why it's right on time, every time.

Martin Luther, a prominent figure in the Protestant Reformation, held a deep conviction that the Word of God is true and powerful. He viewed Scripture as the speech of God, possessing the same creative power that brought the earth into existence. Luther highlights the transformative and comforting power of the active Word of God.

> *Oh! how great and glorious a thing it is to have before one the Word of God! With that we may at all times feel joyous and secure; we need never be in want of consolation, for we see before us, in all its brightness, the pure and right way. He who loses sight of the Word of God, falls into despair; the voice of heaven no longer sustains him; he follows only the disorderly tendency of his heart, and of world vanity, which lead him on to his destruction.*

Does your experience confirm Luther's statement? Mine certainly does. I often lose sight of God, his Word, and the hope he promises.

I take encouragement from the Psalmist who penned the longest Psalm in the Bible. He passionately worships God for 174 verses, celebrating the gift of his Word, and yet, even in the midst of such devotion, he finds himself completely lost. The final verse of the Psalm declares, "I have strayed like a lost sheep, seek your servant" (Ps 119:175). This is hope-giving because it's true to life. I stray so easily and consistently, and if you are anything like me, you may experience the same.

But take heart; God never ceases his pursuit of us, and he does so through his Word. The faith he calls us to embrace and maintain, he creates and sustains through it (Rom 10:17). When the path is shrouded in darkness, God illuminates our way through Scripture (Ps 119:105).

When our hearts are stray from him, he guides and corrects us through what he has written (2 Tim 3:16). In times of weariness and discouragement, he instills us with grit and hope through the Bible (Rom 15:4). In short, he provides us with all we need through his Word.

This includes the training, equipment, and strength that is required of the fight of faith. When Paul talks about going to war with the spiritual forces of darkness, he highlights one offensive weapon: the Word of God (Eph 6:17). Luther loved to talk about the power of God's Word in this context.

He says, "A fiery shield is God's Word; of more substance and purer than gold, which, tried in the fire, loses naught of its substance, but resists and overcomes all the fury of the fiery heat; even so, he that believes God's Word overcomes all, and remains secure everlastingly, against all misfortunes; for this shield fears nothing, neither hell nor the devil." Luther rightly emphasizes the strength, resilience, and ultimate victory found in trusting and living by God's Word.

Scripture is not shy about the transformative power and enduring relevance of God's Word. It is a guiding light, a source of wisdom, and a discerning force that penetrates deep into the human heart. The Word of God is not merely a collection of ancient texts; it is the living, potent, and enduring speech of God that brings light, truth, and change.

Embracing the Word with reverence and trust paves the way to encountering God's presence, discovering solace and guidance, experiencing his assurance, and equipping us for war. Dear reader, we are all on the battlefield; let's take up our weapons.

19

The Most Important Thing About Us

"What comes into our minds when we think about God is the most important thing about us," according to A.W. Tozer. Theology serves as the driving force behind our actions. It shapes how we think and believe, influencing every aspect of our lives.

We are all theologians in some sense, whether we realize it or not. The distinction lies in whether we are good or bad theologians, whether our beliefs align with truth or error, and whether our theology is healthy and beneficial (1 Tim. 1:3-7).

The reach of theology extends far beyond abstract concepts and religious debates. It permeates our daily lives, impacting how we work, how we treat our families, how we interact with our neighbors, and how we navigate relationships (1 Cor. 10:31; Col. 3:17).

Theology informs our perspectives on issues such as war, peace, death, suicide, abuse, money, time, and freedom. Every sphere of life is deeply interconnected with theology, leaving no aspect untouched.

I recall a significant moment during my college years when the subject of the Trinity arose in a class discussion. Confronted with the mind-boggling exploration of how God can exist as one being in three persons, our professor posed a thought-provoking question: "How do we apply the Trinity?" This question aimed to bridge the gap between theology and practicality, urging us to consider how the truth of the Triune God relates to our personal lives, families, and workplaces. It was a truly profound question.

The answer to that question is unequivocal: the Trinity impacts everything. The Triune God serves as the blueprint for true community and authentic relationships (Jn 17:21). In God, we discover the essence of love, service, humility, honor, safety, and acceptance among persons (Jn 17:24, Matt 3:17).

The Trinity reveals how difference and distinction can coexist harmoniously with equality. Probing the mystery of the Trinity, we learn that genuine love is sacrificial and other-centered (Jn 5:23; Phil 2:9-11). The Triune God defines community and relationship, showing us what they truly mean.

Furthermore, the Triune God is the One who saves and redeems us (Rom 1:4; Tit 3:4-7). Our broken relationships and flawed communities stand as evidence of our fallen nature and the need for restoration. All three persons of the Trinity work in perfect unity to accomplish this restoration.

The Father serves as the architect of the rescue mission, sending the Son and the Spirit (Eph. 1:3-14). The Son willingly and humbly pays the ultimate price for our sins and rebellion, while the Spirit empowers the Son's redemptive work and applies its benefits to our lives (Eph. 2:1-10; Gal. 5:22-23).

Through the grace of God, we are drawn into fellowship with the Triune God, experiencing the beauty of true community (1 Jn 1:3; 1 Cor. 1:9). The Trinity revolutionizes our understanding and experience of genuine relationships. Moreover, the Trinity initiates a transformative work within us, enabling us to embody this divine blueprint of community in our homes, workplaces, neighborhoods, and churches (1 Jn 4:7-12).

In essence, the doctrine of the Trinity holds immeasurable potential for practical application. When we contemplate how this profound truth can find tangible expression in our lives, everything changes.

This principle applies to all theological truths. When we explore the implications of the work of the cross, the person of Christ, the person of the Holy Spirit, the nature of humanity, and countless other truths, we open doors to transformative understanding.

Engaging with theology in this manner proves to be deeply enriching and rewarding. When we explore the profound truths of our faith and unearth their practical implications, we witness how these mind-boggling concepts can directly impact the core of our families, jobs, and life challenges. Theology, when embraced and wrestled with, has the power to transform our lives from the inside out.

20

The News We Must Laugh and Be Glad Over

We all love good news, probably because it's rare to receive. That feeling of receiving an unexpected bonus on your paycheck, stumbling upon an unanticipated discount, landing a job promotion, discovering you'll be a grandparent, or hearing your team win on the radio—we cherish good news. The gospel is the best news we can ever receive.

Martin Luther recognized that the gospel is not merely a set of abstract theological concepts, but a powerful message that has the ability to transform lives and bring immeasurable joy.

> *This gospel of God or New Testament is a good story and report, sounded forth into all the world by the apostles, telling of a true David who strove with sin, death, and the devil, and overcame them, and thereby rescued all those who were captive in sin, afflicted with death, and overpowered by the devil. Without any merit of their own he made them righteous, gave them life, and saved them, so that they were given peace and brought back to God...A poor man, dead in sin and consigned to hell, can hear nothing more comforting than this precious and tender message about Christ; from the bottom of his heart, he must laugh and be glad over it, if he believes it true.*

The gospel is not a human invention but a divine proclamation. It is the message of God's triumph over sin, death, and the devil through the person and work of Jesus Christ. This message is not limited to a specific time or place; it resounds throughout history and reaches all corners of the world. Luther's emphasis on the universal nature of the gospel highlights its transformative power for every one of us, regardless of our background, culture, or circumstances.

The gospel is fundamentally about Christ. It reveals God's redemptive plan for humanity, showcasing the sacrificial love of the Father, the atoning work of the Son, and the empowering presence of the Holy Spirit. In the gospel, we witness the great lengths to which God went to rescue and restore us. Through Jesus Christ, the eternal Son of God, the brokenness caused by sin is healed, and a way to reconciliation with God is opened.

The imagery of gospel as a testament or inheritance is particularly poignant. Just as a dying person leaves their possessions to their heirs, Christ, in his sacrificial death, has willed to believers the riches of his life, righteousness, and salvation. Through faith in Christ, believers become recipients of this divine inheritance. We are no longer impoverished by sin and destined for eternal separation from God, but instead, we experience the fullness of life and the assurance of everlasting fellowship with our Creator.

The gospel elicits a response of joy and laughter. It brings an overwhelming sense of gladness and gratitude when we truly grasp its significance. When we recognize the extent of our brokenness and our utter inability to save ourselves, the good news of Christ's victory for us becomes all the more remarkable. In Christ, we find deliverance from the tyranny of sin, liberation from the fear of death, and the promise of eternal life. This realization evokes a deep sense of joy that cannot be contained.

The power of the gospel extends beyond individual salvation to encompass the transformation of relationships and communities. The gospel is not only a personal message of redemption but also the blueprint for true community. Through the Triune God, we witness the perfect love, unity, and self-giving nature that should characterize our relationships. The gospel challenges us to live out this divine model of community, embracing love, service, humility, and honor in our interactions with others.

It is crucial for us to continually reflect on the gospel and allow its transformative power to permeate every aspect of their lives. As we apply the gospel to our relationships, work, and daily challenges, we can experience the radical difference it makes. Good news does not need to be rare in our lives, the message of Christ with its explosive joy awaits us every day.

21

Fear Makes Life Small

The Bible mentions the word "fear" roughly 336 times, highlighting its pervasive presence in Scripture, which mirrors its prevalence in our lives. Extensive research indicates that fear leaves a profound mark on us, affecting our physiological, emotional, mental, and relational health. My life is another data point that confirms this research.

Fear is a reality we cannot escape and must acknowledge, but more importantly, confront. Significantly, within the Bible, there are 70 instances of fear that serve as a call to resist it, emphasizing the importance of not succumbing to fear. Walter Brueggemann provides some helpful insight on what fear does to us.

> *When we live according to our fears and our hates, our lives become small and defensive, lacking the deep, joyous generosity of God. If you find some part of your life where your daily round has grown thin and controlling and resentful, life with God is much, much larger, shattering our little categories of control, permitting us to say that God's purposes led us well beyond ourselves to live and to forgive, to create life we would not have imagined.*

This quote beautifully captures the profound impact that fear and hate can have on our lives. When we allow these negative emotions to dictate our actions, we become trapped in a small, defensive existence. It's as if we build walls around ourselves, restricting our capacity to experience the deep and joyous generosity of life.

The mention of living with God highlights the transformative power of faith and spirituality. It suggests that by embracing a broader perspective and acknowledging a higher purpose, we can break free from the constraints of our fears and resentments. In doing so, we open ourselves to a more expansive, forgiving, and creative life that surpasses our limited expectations.

The idea that God's purposes can lead us beyond our narrow confines reminds us that there is a greater plan at work, and it often involves taking us on unexpected journeys. It's a call to let go of control, to embrace the unknown, and to trust in the possibility of a life that we couldn't have imagined on our own.

Brueggemann's insights on the effects of fear resonate with biblical teachings. The Bible repeatedly emphasizes the significance of overcoming fear and embracing God's expansive and transformative love. Paul writes, "For God has not given us a spirit of fear, but of power and of love and of a sound mind" (2 Tim 1:7). Fear is not from God, but rather, he desires to empower us with love, strength, and a sound mind to face life's challenges with confidence and courage.

Moreover, the psalmist encourages us, "When I am afraid, I put my trust in you" (Ps 56:30). The remedy for fear is entrusting ourselves to God, recognizing his ability to provide us with comfort, guidance, and a sense of security. This call to action is underpinned by the promise that, as we confront our fears, we will encounter the supporting presence of God: "Fear not, for I am with you; be not dismayed, for I am your God; I will strengthen you, I will help you, I will uphold you with my righteous right hand" (Is 41:10).

The transformative power of God's love is beautifully expressed by John, "There is no fear in love. But perfect love drives out fear because fear has to do with punishment. The one who fears is not made perfect in love" (1 Jn 4:18). When we immerse ourselves in God's perfect love, fear loses its grip on our lives.

This love, demonstrated at the cross, will chase down and ruthlessly eliminate the fears in our souls concerning God's present and ultimate disposition towards us. If this love can uproot such profound fear, it is undoubtedly capable of dispelling all lesser fears. It is through experiencing God's unconditional love that we find freedom from fear and can embrace a life of love, generosity, and forgiveness.

The recurring theme of fear in Scripture serves as a reminder that we will continually confront it in our lives. In those moments when your soul trembles and anxiety takes hold, remember that you are not alone. Take to heart God's call to action and his promise: "Have I not commanded you? Be strong and courageous. Do not be frightened, and do not be dismayed, for the Lord your God is with you wherever you go" (Josh 1:9). Take this truth and go to war.

22

The Youthfulness of God: Learning from our Kids

Children are the best teachers; they often reveal aspects of life we've forgotten. They possess an innate ability to grasp the essence of matters, live in the present, nurture authentic relationship, and marvel at the world's wonders. Fyodor Dostoyevsky, renowned Russian novelist, once remarked: "The soul is healed by being with children."

G.K. Chesterton, author and theologian, perhaps best captured the connection between the wonder of children and the heart of God.

> *Because children have abounding vitality, because they are in spirit fierce and free, therefore they want things repeated and unchanged. They always say, "Do it again;" and the grown-up person does it again until he is nearly dead. For grown-up people are not strong enough to exult in monotony. But perhaps God is strong enough to exult in monotony. It is possible that God says every morning, "Do it again" to the sun; and every evening, "Do it again" to the moon. It may not be automatic necessity that makes all daisies alike; it may be that God makes every daisy separately, but has never got tired of making them. It may be that he has the eternal appetite of infancy; for we have sinned and grown old, and our Father is younger than we.*

I'm fascinated by how this quote exposes lesser-known aspects of God's character. Chesterton is right, children are a window into the heart of God. While we age and succumb to weariness, God grows younger—he possesses an everlasting appetite for the wonder of creation that surpasses our comprehension. Children with their unbounded vitality and untamed spirits are a profound reflection of God. What else do we have to learn from children?

The concept of embracing childlikeness is a recurring theme in both biblical teachings and the insights of theologians. Scripture affirms the inherent goodness of childlike qualities such as humility, dependence, and simple faith. Karl Rahner extends this understanding by stating, "Childhood is not a state which only applies to the first phase of our lives in the biological sense. Rather it is a basic condition which is always appropriate to a life that is lived aright."

C.S. Lewis, in his thought-provoking perspective, equates maturity and adulthood with the willingness to embrace an appropriate level of childishness.

> *Critics who treat "adult" as a term of approval, instead of as a merely descriptive term, cannot be adult themselves. To be concerned about being grown up, to admire the grown up because it is grown up, to blush at the suspicion of being childish; these things are the marks of childhood and adolescence. And in childhood and adolescence they are, in moderation, healthy symptoms. Young things ought to want to grow. But to carry on into middle life or even into early manhood this concern about being adult is a mark of really arrested development. When I was ten, I read fairy tales in secret and would have been ashamed if I had been found doing so. Now that I am fifty I read them openly. When I became a man I put away childish things, including the fear of childishness and the desire to be very grown up.*

This perspective encourages us to reevaluate our perception of adulthood and maturity. It challenges the notion that growing up entails abandoning childlike qualities altogether. Instead, it emphasizes that true maturity involves embracing childlike attributes such as wonder, imagination, and a willingness to see the world with fresh eyes. Jesus himself affirmed the importance of childlike faith, "Truly, I say to you, unless you turn and become like children, you will never enter the kingdom of heaven" (Matt 18:3).

Therefore, the call to childlikeness extends beyond a specific phase in life; it is a continuous disposition that allows us to approach God and the world with humility, dependence, and steady faith. As we embrace childlikeness, we tap into the beauty of simplicity, curiosity, and openness that fosters spiritual growth, deepens our relationship with God, and enriches our experience of the world around us. As Jesus said, we must "become like children."

The God of Encouragement

Among the items found in Abraham Lincoln's wallet at the time of his death were a Confederate five-dollar bill and eight newspaper clippings. These clippings were extracted from newspapers published just before Lincoln's assassination and featured complimentary remarks about him that had been written during his campaign for re-election to the presidency. In other words, all he had was money and encouragement in his wallet.

Encouragement matters significantly, whether it's the cheering voice at the end of a marathon, the comforting words after a challenging workday, a letter of affirmation from a loved one, or a newspaper clipping that honors your efforts. Encouragement is a remarkable force that often goes underestimated in our lives.

Its impact is profound, as it has the ability to redirect our paths, shape our future, overshadow our past, and infuse our present with courage. The Bible calls us to engage in the important work of instilling hope in others through encouragement.

To do so effectively, it is crucial to develop a biblical framework that guides our thinking and practice of encouragement. When we consider the most encouraging character in the Bible, one individual stands out prominently: Barnabas. In fact, he was so remarkably encouraging that he was given the nickname "the son of encouragement." Yet, it is important to note that Barnabas serves as a mere reflection, a faint echo of the greatest encourager.

To construct a solid framework for encouragement, we must start with a strong foundation. Romans 15:5-6 provides a significant starting point for our discussion: "May the God of endurance and encouragement grant you to live in such harmony with one another, in accord with Christ Jesus, that together you may with one voice glorify the God and Father of our Lord Jesus Christ."

In this verse, encouragement is not just a sporadic action of God; it describes his very character and nature. It reveals that God is the encouraging God himself, continuously and consistently offering encouragement. This goes beyond occasional acts of encouragement; it represents a posture, a way of existence, and a way of interaction.

The entirety of Scripture tells the story of a God who encourages, infuses hope, and instills courage. Consider the encouraging walks with God in the garden or the comforting response to the original rebellion through clothing and the promise of a Savior (Gen 3:8, 21).

Think about the safety found in the ark and the assurance symbolized by the rainbow, assuring that the earth will never be flooded again (Gen 9:13-16). Recall the promise and birth of Isaac, the deliverance in the Exodus, the fulfillment of entering the promised land, the provision of the tabernacle and temple, the rise of righteous leaders, the comforting words of the prophets, and the promises of a coming Messiah.

The encouraging God reveals himself fully in the incarnation when Christ walks among us in human form. In Christ, we witness the embodiment of divine encouragement. We see it through his words and actions recorded in the gospels. As we read the gospels and observe Christ's interactions, encouragement emanates from his very being. Moreover, the ultimate source of encouragement is found in the good news of the gospel, the message of the death and resurrection of Jesus for our rescue.

The New Testament concludes with an outpouring of encouragement. It speaks of the return of Christ, the hope for the future, the promise of a new heavens and new earth, the end of sorrow, the eternal presence of God, and an everlasting abundance of hope. At the core of all encouragement lies our Creator, God himself. He is the ultimate encourager, and all encouragement flows from his heart and his actions.

24

Mirror and Neighbor: Encouragement Under our Noses

Consider this extraordinary truth: out of all of creation, you are the only one that caused God to pause, stoop down into the dirt, carefully shape you, and breathe life into your being. You alone bear the image of God. No other creature, whether animal or angel, shares this privilege. At the moment of creation, God declared you as "very good" (Gen 1:31). This initial act of encouragement from our Creator signifies his intention and delight in creating you in his image.

Being an image-bearer means holding immense value and being a source of joy to God. It involves being endowed with unique qualities, gifts, and attributes specific to you. There is only one you. The image of God is a truth that encourages and uplifts. Moreover, it forms the foundation for mutual encouragement.

James reinforces the significance of recognizing the image of God in others: "With our tongue we bless our Lord and Father, and with it we curse people who are made in the likeness of God. From the same mouth come blessing and cursing. My brothers, these things ought not to be so" (Jas 3:9). Cursing someone who bears the image of God is completely contrary to what should be done.

Blessing, encouraging, and building up others is the only appropriate response to fellow image-bearers. When we align our perspective towards one another with God's perspective, a transformative shift occurs. Every human being on this planet possesses intrinsic value and dignity. The image of God in each individual calls us to the important task of affirmation. God's encouragement has been right in front of us all along, both in the mirror and in our neighbors.

Encouragement is the intentional act of one image-bearer directing their gaze towards another, recognizing and affirming the qualities that God has placed within them. Consider the unique gifts, talents, skills, personality traits, character, and perspectives that each individual possesses.

If we view one another through the right lenses, there is an abundance to appreciate and celebrate. This principle applies to ourselves as well. When we look into the mirror, it's a time for expressing gratitude for God's handiwork.

Encouragement goes beyond mere observation; it involves active affirmation. When we witness acts of mercy, patience, kindness, joy, strength, or compassion in someone, encouragement verbalizes what is seen and affirms the individual. When we recognize gifts and skills, we validate them. Encouragement acknowledges the reflection of God in each image-bearer and reminds them of the truth about who they are.

Being an image-bearer is an uplifting reality. To encourage others is to embody the role of a good image-bearer, reflecting the nature of the great Encourager himself. The image of God in others invites us to see God in them and to affirm what we see.

Rescued from Wrath: The Encouragement of the Cross

As Martin Luther famously proclaimed, "the cross alone is our theology." It is essential to center our thinking on all theological matters around the cross. Every aspect of our understanding must be woven through the lens of the cross for true comprehension. The cross of Jesus Christ represents the pinnacle of God's self-revelation. It is the Mount Everest of his self-disclosure, the place where we glimpse the very heart of God.

The cross reveals the salvation of God, making it the epitome of encouragement. Consider Paul's words, "For God has not destined us for wrath, but to obtain salvation through our Lord Jesus Christ, who died for us so that whether we are awake or asleep we might live with him. Therefore, encourage one another and build one another up, just as you are doing" (1 Thess 5:9-11).

These verses present two dimensions of gospel encouragement. First, it provides encouragement in the face of judgment and wrath. Dear reader, the most significant problem we face in this world is the wrath and judgment of God. It is not the devil or even our sin. It is God's righteous response to our sin that poses the greatest challenge (Rom 1:18; 6:23).

The God of Encouragement is a pure and holy God, infinitely above all. He cannot and will not tolerate evil. His heart grieves over the sins of humanity, and He is furious about it (Gen 6:5-7). His anger is not capricious or unpredictable like our human anger (Num 23:19). David Peterson aptly describes God's wrath as a "fixed and determined response to all that is unholy and evil." It is the just response to wickedness. To act otherwise would compromise his integrity, his goodness, and his justice.

Hell is a reality, and it is not a domain where Satan reigns. Rather, it is a place where God executes judgment and pours out eternal wrath (Matt 10:28; 2 Thess 1:9). This truth reveals the depths of our sin and underscores the offensive nature of our rebellion.

In order to comprehend the magnitude of God's love for us in the gospel, we must grasp the depths of our sin and the impending judgment of God (Rom 5:20-21). The text assures us that those who have placed their trust in Christ are not destined for wrath but for salvation (Jn 10:28).

Jesus Christ came and took our place. He became our wrath-quencher, bearing upon his shoulders the full weight of God's judgment (Rom 3:24-25). At Calvary, wave after wave of God's righteous wrath crashed upon him, and he absorbed and exhausted it all (1 Jn 2:1-2). At the cross, the judgment of God was completed and fulfilled (Jn 19:30).

To illustrate this truth, imagine a firefighter who rushes into a burning house while the flames are about to consume you. He steps in front of the flames, removes his fireproof jacket, covers you with it, and endures the flames in your place. The biblical term for this gospel truth is propitiation—the wrath-quenching love of Christ (1 Jn 4:10). This means that for those hidden in Christ, there is no longer any wrath or judgment awaiting them.

This leads us to the second aspect of gospel encouragement in the verse above: we have encouragement for all of life, including the face of death. Whether we live or die, we belong to Christ. This is an unchanging reality. He is propitious toward us, forever favorably disposed.

Paul declares that the gospel ensures we will "always live with him." We are his, and he dwells with us even now. And when we face death, we will dwell with him under his roof. The gospel is the sole hope in the face of death, a firm and unwavering confidence that our Creator is for us and will carry us through life and into eternity.

The text concludes by urging us to encourage one another with these words. Lift up your head, dear Christian. Let your hearts soar! Our judgment is no more! Embrace the encouragement found in the cross, for it is our hope, assurance, and guarantee of an eternal future.

26

You are Not an Island: Encouragement and Community

In a recent study conducted in the United States, a therapeutic research group found the following concerning statistics: 52% reported feeling lonely, 47% indicated that their relationships lacked meaning, 58% stated that nobody truly knows them, and 57% reported eating all their meals alone.

The issue of loneliness in our country is so alarming that even the Surgeon General identified it as a mental health hazard in a recent report, stating, "Our epidemic of loneliness and isolation has been an underappreciated public health crisis that has harmed both individual and societal health."

When God fashioned us, he created us in his image. It's essential to remember that God has always existed in community, as the Trinity. To be made in his image, in part, means being designed for community.

This truth becomes evident when we consider that God declared everything in his creation good and perfect after completing his work, with one exception: "It is not good for the man to be alone" (Gen 2:18). We cannot escape it; we are inherently wired for others, for community, for a sense of belonging.

The work of Christ is about transforming those of us who were not his people into his people. "But you are a chosen race, a royal priesthood, a holy nation, a people for his own possession, that you may proclaim the excellencies of him who called you out of darkness into his marvelous light. Once you were not a people, but now you are God's people; once you had not received mercy, but now you have received mercy" (1 Pet 2:9-10). By his mercy, we belong.

The presence of God's people in the world serves as an immense source of encouragement. Gathering together, we find encouragement, and it's our calling to bring that encouragement to the world. The book of Hebrews emphasizes the importance of encouragement in safeguarding one another and fostering perseverance in the faith.

For example, the author says: "Take care, brothers, lest there be in any of you an evil, unbelieving heart, leading you to fall away from the living God. But encourage one another every day, as long as it is called 'today,' that none of you may be hardened by the deceitfulness of sin" (Heb 3:13).

The slippery slope of unbelief, hardness of heart, and drifting away from God is a reality that we all face. Countless times, I have entered a Sunday morning church service with a heart hardened like a rock. I have experienced the inclination towards unbelief and callousness.

However, I have also felt the softening touch of God's Spirit through the encouragement of my brothers and sisters in Christ. We genuinely need one another. Encouragement is specifically designed to shatter the stony hearts that can easily overtake us.

In 1 Thessalonians 5:14, Paul instructs us to "encourage the fainthearted." The term "fainthearted" conveys the idea of being "little souled." It describes the condition where circumstances, pain, suffering, and discouragement deflate us, shrinking our capacity for hope.

Encouragement breathes hope into our hearts, expanding the confines of our souls once more. It revitalizes our ability to hope. This is precisely what happens when we gather together and encourage one another. When we communicate the promises of the gospel to each other repeatedly, our capacity for hope is restored and enlarged.

The truth is, we need one another. Life is not meant to be a solitary pursuit; it's a communal endeavor where we come alongside each other, lifting one another up and infusing hope into each other's lives. Easier said than done, yes, I agree. We've all experienced pain, hurt, and disillusionment in our church experiences, and, if we're honest, we've potentially caused pain for others as well.

That being said, the solution is not isolation; it's fostering rhino skin and pressing on. It's about being discerning and finding the people you can trust, and they are out there. It's okay if it's only one or two; that's wisdom: "A man of many companions may come to ruin, but there is a friend who sticks closer than a brother" (Prov 18:24).

In the end, my friends, we must push past the hurt and isolation. You can't do it alone; you were never intended to. And God has provided for you so you don't have to.

27

Last Chapter, Best Chapter: The Hope of Christ's Return

Billy Graham says this about the return of Jesus: "The second coming of Christ will be so revolutionary that it will change every aspect of life on this planet. Christ will reign in righteousness. Disease will be arrested. Death will be modified. War will be abolished. Nature will be changed. Man will live as he was originally intended to live."

This is a hope-giving thought. Not surprisingly, the New Testament explicitly links encouragement to Christ's second coming. This is particularly evident in 1 Thessalonians 4:14-18:

> *For since we believe that Jesus died and rose again, even so, through Jesus, God will bring with him those who have fallen asleep. For this, we declare to you by a word from the Lord, that we who are alive, who are left until the coming of the Lord, will not precede those who have fallen asleep. For the Lord himself will descend from heaven with a cry of command, with the voice of an archangel, and with the sound of the trumpet of God. And the dead in Christ will rise first. Then we who are alive, who are left, will be caught up together with them in the clouds to meet the Lord in the air, and so we will always be with the Lord. Therefore, encourage one another with these words.*

The final sentence says it all: these words about Christ's future return provide sustaining courage for the challenges of today. Paul's explanation of the second coming provides a firm foundation for our hope and encouragement. It is certain that the same Jesus who bore the wrath of God to rescue us will return to gather those who have placed their trust in him.

This future event is so certain that Graeme Goldsworthy beautifully described it as "future history." It is certain that we will receive a renewed, resurrected body at the time of his coming. His return signals the end of sickness, sorrow, and death.

Moreover, it is certain we will be reunited with fellow believers who have passed away before us. When Jesus returns, we will be with him forever. He will not leave us as orphans; he will come for us. This assurance is a cause for great encouragement.

In the midst of the pain of this fallen world, we can find solace in the knowledge that this is as bad as it gets. On the other hand, if we reject Christ, this present life represents the best we will ever experience. As we trust Jesus, we can take heart because things will absolutely get better. This is not the final chapter of the story.

It is crucial not to succumb to the lie that life is limited to this temporary existence. We must remember that we have eternal life, and the last chapter is the best chapter. Every disappointment, crushed dream, and unmet expectation will be overshadowed by a life that will never end.

This is a certainty that will never disappoint—a rare situation where you should put all your "eggs in one basket." That's why Peter tells us, "set your hope fully on the grace that will be brought to you at the revelation of Jesus Christ" (1 Pet 1:13). Dear reader, you can put the full weight of expectation on his return.

Contaminated By Responsible Action

"This is the end—for me, the beginning of life." These were the final words of a young German pastor who resisted Hitler's dark regime and was hanged for it. Dietrich Bonhoeffer, a theologian who lived during that challenging historical period, found himself grappling with Hitler's dictatorship and the horrors of the Holocaust.

In his role as a Christ-follower, pastor, and professor, he faced the dilemma of how to respond to such an impossible context. Rather than turning a blind eye, Bonhoeffer actively embodied and promoted a different approach. His words offer profound wisdom and pose a challenging question to all of us.

> *Here and there people flee from public altercation into the sanctuary of private virtuousness. But anyone who does this must shut his mouth and his eyes to the injustice around him. Only at the cost of self-deception can he keep himself pure from the contamination arising from responsible action. In spite of all that he does, what he leaves undone will rob him of his peace of mind. He will either go to pieces because of the disquiet, or become the most hypocritical of Pharisees. Who stands fast? Only the man whose final standard is not his reason, his principles. his conscience, his freedom, or his virtue, but who is ready to sacrifice all this when he is called to obedient and responsible action in faith and in exclusive allegiance to God---the responsible man, who tries to make his whole life an answer to the question and call of God. Where are these responsible people?*

Dietrich Bonhoeffer's example of opposing Hitler offers profound lessons for Christians today in navigating the complexities of moral and ethical responsibility in a troubled world.

Courageous Engagement. Bonhoeffer's life teaches us the importance of active and courageous engagement in the face of injustice. While it may be tempting to withdraw into a cocoon of personal piety or convince ourselves that it's not our problem, we are called to confront the injustices around us (Mic 6:8; Is 1:17).

This means taking a stand and speaking out against oppression, even when it's uncomfortable or risky. In our current world, where various forms of injustice persist, we are called to advocate for those who cannot speak for themselves, just as Bonhoeffer did (Prov 31:8-9).

Embracing Contamination. Contamination, getting one's hands dirty, and enduring discomfort are the necessary, albeit challenging, consequences of responsible action. As we engage with the world's injustices and confront moral dilemmas, we may find ourselves in situations where our principles are put to the test, potentially leading to a sense of moral discomfort and contamination.

However, it is vital to understand that these challenges are an inherent part of the journey towards justice and serving God. In the pursuit of such noble goals, our primary allegiance should always be to God's call, even when it leads us through muddy waters. Bonhoeffer highlights that the practical wisdom of embracing the messiness and discomfort as part and parcel of responsible action, emphasizing that, in the end, remaining committed to our faith and God's call is of utmost importance, regardless of the difficulties encountered along the way (1 Cor 4:9-13, 9:19-23).

A Life of Sacrificial Commitment. Bonhoeffer's unwavering dedication to the call of God reminds us that being responsible is not a one-time endeavor. It's a lifelong pursuit. This enduring commitment to obedient and responsible action, even at the cost of personal comfort, challenges us to put our faith into action. He challenges us to be willing to sacrifice our comfort and privilege when the call to serve God and address injustice is paramount (2 Cor 8:9).

Responsible action is far from easy; it compels us to prioritize the needs of others over our personal desires, a life posture that mirrors the example of Jesus (Phil 2:3-11).

Bonhoeffer's challenge remains relevant today. We must resist the temptation to withdraw into our private sanctuaries of virtue, disconnected from the world's problems. Instead, we are called to embrace the messiness of responsible action, sacrificing our own comfort and reputation for the sake of justice and obedience to God.

(29)

Unexpected Majesty: The Maker of Man Becomes One

The Christmas story is unlike any other, filled with unlikely and unexpected twists and turns. The sleepy town of Bethlehem, the choice of a virgin for God's incarnation, a humble stable as the birthplace of the King of Kings, surrounded by a crowd of animals and humble shepherds—these aspects seem to contradict the grand promises of a Savior who would reign and rule with might and majesty, the one who was destined to save and shepherd his people. Yet, this is precisely the unique and extraordinary entrance that God, in his wisdom, chose for his Son.

As we step back and contemplate the nativity, we come to realize that Christmas is not only about God's saving work but also about his revealing work. It is a divine autobiography, where God chooses to unveil himself to the world, showing us who he truly is and what he is like. The majesty of God displayed in this story is unexpected, defying human expectations and revealing his incomprehensible love for humanity.

This revelation of God's majesty is witnessed in the humility, passion, and generosity displayed in the nativity. We see the Creator of all things taking his first breath as a vulnerable newborn baby, wrapped in swaddling clothes and lying in a manger, an epitome of humility. The prophet Isaiah's words in Isaiah 9:6 ring true as we grasp the wonder of this paradox: "For to us, a child is born, to us, a son is given; and the government shall be upon his shoulder, and his name shall be called Wonderful Counselor, Mighty God, Everlasting Father, Prince of Peace."

In John 1:14, we read, "And the Word became flesh and dwelt among us, and we have seen his glory, glory as of the only Son from the Father, full of grace and truth." This passage emphasizes the glory and majesty of God made manifest in the humble form of a human being, the Son of God becoming the Son of Man. The words of Augustine in one of his Christmas sermons further illuminate this profound truth:

The Word of the Father, by whom all time was created, was made flesh and was born In time for us. He, without whose divine permission no day completes its course, wished to have one day set aside for his human birth. In the bosom of his Father, he existed before all the cycles of ages; born of an earthly mother, he entered upon the course of the years on this day. The Maker of man became man that he, Ruler of the stars, might be nourished at the breast; that he, the Bread, might be hungry; that he, the Fountain, might thirst; that he, the Light, might sleep; that he, the Way, might be wearied by the journey; that he, the Truth, might be accused by false witnesses; that he, the Judge of the living and the dead, might be brought to trial by a mortal judge; that he, Justice, might be condemned by the unjust; that he, the Foundation, might be suspended upon a cross; that Courage might be weakened; that Security might be wounded; that Life might die.

The nativity story, therefore, challenges our preconceived notions of greatness and grandeur. It is a reminder that true majesty is found in humility, selflessness, and sacrificial love. Jesus, the King of Kings, was not born in a palace but in a humble stable. He willingly chose to embrace the limitations of human existence to identify with his creation and redeem humanity.

May the joy of the angels who proclaimed his birth, the gratitude of the shepherds who welcomed him into the world, and the persistence and wisdom of the Magi who diligently sought him with their whole hearts inspire us to seek more of God in our lives. Friends, take joy in God's unexpected majesty and his unending love for you.

Own It: Living a Life of Persistent Repentance

"Of all acts of man repentance is the most divine. The greatest of all faults is to be conscious of none," says Thomas Carlyle. Repentance and faith are two vital aspects of the Christian life, both rooted in ownership and radical acceptance of God's truth.

Repentance involves owning our sin, acknowledging our failures, rebellion, and transgressions before God. It is a humble recognition that we have fallen short of God's glory and a full acceptance of our responsibility in our wrongdoing.

Matthew 4:17 emphasizes that repentance is not just a one-time event but a continuous lifestyle and posture for followers of Christ. In essence, the entire life of believers is to be one of repentance. To embrace repentance is to take a sincere and humble stance, confessing our sins before God, seeking his forgiveness, and turning away from our old ways.

As the Psalmist expressed in Psalm 51:17, "The sacrifices of God are a broken spirit; a broken and contrite heart, O God, you will not despise." This brokenness and contrition in repentance allow us to open ourselves to God's transforming grace and mercy.

On the other hand, faith also requires ownership, but it focuses on grasping onto God's promises and accepting his righteousness imparted to us through Christ. It involves trusting in the finished work of Christ on the cross, where our condemnation was settled once and for all. Faith allows us to lean on the certainty of our future, knowing that we will have an unending, resurrected existence as heirs of God's promises.

As Paul beautifully expresses in Romans 4:20-22, "No unbelief made him waver concerning the promise of God, but he grew strong in his faith as he gave glory to God, fully convinced that God was able to do what he had promised. That is why his faith was counted to him as righteousness."

To possess faith is to take hold of God's gracious gift of salvation and confidently trust in his grace. It is not a passive belief but an active, living confidence in God's love and favor. As Luther aptly describes, faith is "a living, daring confidence in God's grace, so sure and certain that a man would stake his life on it a thousand times."

In the Christian life, radical ownership is required. We wholeheartedly acknowledge our sinfulness and take full responsibility for it, embracing God's provision for forgiveness and restoration through Christ. We own our brokenness and find healing in repentance, while simultaneously grasping onto God's promises, confidently taking hold of Christ's righteousness through faith.

In sum, repentance and faith are not mutually exclusive; rather, they are complementary expressions of radical ownership. They are the foundations of the Christian life, shaping our relationship with God and transforming us into the image of Christ.

Furthermore, these are not one-time actions but rather persistent, ongoing postures required by our need for grace and the gospel. The fight of faith is also a battle to lead a life of repentance, continuously moving from darkness into the light, and fully taking ownership of ourselves before God.

The Freedom to Forget Yourself

The ancient Greek myth of Narcissus tells a powerful story of self-absorption and the tragic consequences of an inward-focused existence. Narcissus, a strikingly handsome young man, captivated all who laid eyes on him, but he paid little attention to the adoration of others. One fateful day, while he wandered through the woods, he came upon a clear, tranquil pool of water.

As he bent down to drink, he caught sight of his own reflection and was immediately ensnared by its beauty. He became utterly infatuated with the image, unable to tear himself away from his own reflection. He wasted away, consumed by his obsession with himself, until all that remained was the echo of his name.

The tale of Narcissus serves as a timeless cautionary tale, emphasizing the perils of excessive self-love and self-absorption. It stands in stark contrast to our divine design, which encourages us to direct our gaze outward, to see and care for the world and the people around us, fostering connections and selfless relationships that lead to a life of purpose, joy, and freedom.

God, in his divine design, fashioned us with the capacity to see the world and the people around us, but not ourselves. Our eyes were intended to look outward, focusing on others and our Maker. Genesis 1-2 beautifully portrays humanity looking upward to God and outward to his creation. Adam and Eve's purpose was to care for each other, the living creatures, and the earth, embodying an other-focused and outward-postured vocation.

However, Genesis 3 marks a tragic turning point in human history. Our rebellion against God was an inward turn, driven by self-concern, pursuit of personal desires, and an exaltation of our own understanding of reality. In that moment, self-preservation and self-concern took precedence, and humanity's focus shifted from the "other" to the self. In short, sin transformed the myth of Narcissus into a sorrowful reality. This self-centeredness defined humanity, and we became enslaved to ourselves, neglecting the service and love we were made for.

Romans 1:18-32 outlines the judgment that rests upon humanity due to our self-devotion and the exploitation of others. Sin is not an abstract concept but deeply personal. It affects real people with real names, and it offends the Triune God. Our self-centered actions grieve our Creator and harm our fellow human beings.

Repentance demands that we take full responsibility for the brokenness and damage caused by sin in our lives. It is a movement back towards the Creator, agreeing with his assessment of our misplaced loyalties. The psalmist's cry in Psalm 41:4 becomes our plea: "Lord, have mercy on me, heal me, for I have sinned against you."

The beauty of God's redemptive plan unfolds through the person of Christ. In Jesus Christ, we witness humanity's true design. Christ looks upward to his Father and outward to his fractured creation.

As the outward-postured God, he rescues us from the consequences of our self-worship. The judgment we earned for ourselves is borne by the Son of God, the one true worshiper of the Father. Jesus Christ, the free God who willingly bound himself to the cross, shatters the chains of self-slavery and offers us true freedom.

In other words, the gospel frees us from ourselves: "For the love of Christ controls us, because we have concluded this: that one has died for all, therefore all have died; and he died for all, that those who live might no longer live for themselves but for him who for their sake died and was raised" (2 Cor 5:14-15). Freed from self-absorption, the gospel directs us back to God's initial blueprint for humanity.

The saving work of the Triune God surpasses mere forgiveness, cleansing, and restoring our right standing before him. He does not leave us in our brokenness but gives us new hearts and places the

Holy Spirit within us. He transforms our inward curve to bend outward once more.

The Triune God is wholly devoted to restoring what was lost, remaking what was broken, and leading us into the freedom of living for others. Through this transformation, we find our true humanity, being drawn into the divine dance of selfless love, unity, and otherness within the Trinity.

A Million Boring Little Things

"What I need courage for is the ordinary, the daily every-dayness of life. Caring for a homeless kid is a lot more thrilling to me than listening well to the people in my home. Giving away clothes and seeking out edgy Christian communities requires less of me than being kind to my wife on an average Wednesday morning or calling my mom back when I don't feel like it," says author Michael Horton.

Walking with Jesus is about faithfulness in the mundane. Richard Beck, theology professor at Abilene Christian University, argued that the Christian life is made up of a million boring little things.

What no one ever shares with you when you're young is that Christianity is boring. No one tells you that Christianity is a 70–80-year grind in becoming more kind, more gentle, more giving, more joyful, more patient, more loving. You learn that God isn't in the rocking praise band or the amped up worship experience. What you learn after college is that Holy Ground is standing patiently in a line. You learn that holy ground is learning to listen well to your child, wife or co-worker. Holy ground is being a reliable and unselfish friend or family member and being a good nurse when someone is sick. Holy ground is awkward and unlikely friendships. Holy ground is often just showing up. Being more and more like Jesus is a million boring little things. No one ever tells you that when you're young. Just like no one ever tells you just how risky and revolutionary it all is. That a truly radical life of following Jesus is made up of a million boring little things.

Beck offers a candid perspective on the often-overlooked facets of faith. The initial allure of vibrant worship experiences and dynamic events can overshadow the quieter, less flashy aspects of living out one's faith. The notion that Christianity is a "70–80-year grind" underscores the long-term, everyday commitment it entails.

The reflection sheds light on the transformational nature of the Christian life, emphasizing that it's not about the sensational moments but rather a continual process of becoming more compassionate, patient, and loving. It challenges the perception that God is exclusively found in grand, emotionally charged settings, redirecting attention to the sacredness of seemingly mundane situations.

The concept of holy ground being found in everyday scenarios, such as patiently waiting in line or attentively listening to loved ones, redefines the spiritual landscape. It highlights the holiness inherent in acts of kindness, reliability, and selflessness.

This perspective underscores the beauty of ordinary, daily interactions as opportunities for spiritual growth and connection with the divine. This truth tracks with the biblical call to mundanity: "Aspire to live quietly, and to mind your own affairs, and to work with your hands, as we instructed you, so that you may walk properly before outsiders and be dependent on no one (1 Thess 4:11-12).

Such thoughts prompt a reevaluation of the Christian faith, encouraging an appreciation for the "million boring little things" that collectively contribute to becoming more Christ-like. It challenges the expectation that Christianity should always be thrilling, emphasizing that true radicalism is often manifested in consistent, unremarkable acts of love and service. Overall, it is a reminder that the depth of a Christian life lies in the commitment to the small.

33

The Alphabet of Pain, the Language of Sorrow

"He is a bear lying in wait for me, a lion in hiding; he turned aside my steps and tore me to pieces; he has made me desolate; he bent his bow and set me as a target for his arrow. He drove into my kidneys the arrows of his quiver" (Lam 3:10-13). I'm guessing you've never heard this prayer read aloud in a church service. It's regrettable that such passages are infrequently integrated into the life of faith, considering they are precisely the resources we need in our pain.

The inclusion of the book of Lamentations in the Bible serves as a profound reminder of God's compassion and understanding towards human suffering. This collection of poetic laments, written in the aftermath of Jerusalem's destruction, gives voice to the raw emotions of grief, pain, and despair experienced by the people of Israel. Through this book, we witness a powerful expression of human vulnerability, where individuals pour out their hearts to God in moments of intense suffering.

Lamentations was written in the face of devastation, serving as a biblical manual for grief—a guiding compass in our sorrow, a voice for the indescribable groans and unspeakable pain we endure. In each of the initial four chapters, Jeremiah employs a Hebrew acrostic, traversing the Hebrew alphabet repeatedly as he pours out his lament before God.

This book embodies an acrostic of grief, introducing us to the alphabet of pain, granting us a language for sorrow. It becomes a resonant voice amid our suffering. Furthermore, the structure of this book emphasizes the significance of intentional grieving. It takes the tumultuous chaos of pain and loss and imbues it with order and purpose. There's a deliberate attempt to exhaust the expression of sorrow, from A to Z, working through the depths of loss and offering a complete outlet for grief.

Lamentations teaches us that it is not only acceptable but also essential to bring our deepest struggles and sorrows before God. This act of lament is an authentic and courageous way of engaging with our Creator in times of distress. It demonstrates that God desires a genuine relationship with his people, where we can be honest about our pain and seek his comfort and guidance. In these verses, we find a safe space to express our doubts, fears, and questions, without fear of judgment or rejection.

The beauty of Lamentations lies in the truth that it reflects the reality of human life. It acknowledges that suffering is an unavoidable part of our existence. It doesn't sugarcoat the harsh realities of life or offer quick fixes. Instead, it provides a space for lament, acknowledging the brokenness of the world while inviting us to trust in the faithfulness and goodness of God even in the midst of adversity.

Through the cries of lament, we witness the unshakable hope that emerges from the depths of despair (Lam 3:22-23). The book shows that even in the darkest times, God's love and compassion endure. It reminds us that we are not alone in our pain, for God himself suffers with us. He is not distant or indifferent to our struggles but is intimately involved in our lives, holding us close to his heart.

In the midst of loss and devastation, one thing remains constant: our voice. Lamentations shows us that even when everything else is stripped away, we still have the ability to cry out, petition, and lament. God has bound himself to us through a covenant that guarantees his ear will hear our cries. He listens to us; it is his commitment to hear and respond to his people in their pain and suffering.

Throughout history, we see this unwavering voice in the cries of Israel during their slavery in Egypt, in the anguished lament of Job, and in the exiled people of God. However, the most profound example is found in Jesus, the carpenter outside the walls of Jerusalem. He was stripped of everything, except his voice. The cry of forsakenness from the cross boldly refused to be silenced (Mk 15:34).

In this book, we witness the gift of God as he authors the words that reflect our human experience. He understands our frame, our limits, and our needs. Through Lamentations, God instructs us in the way of pain and suffering and invites us into a bold dialogue with him. He gives us the language to express our deepest grief and pain.

In life, pain is inevitable. But the pathway through pain to peace and rest is not guaranteed. It is easy to succumb to bitterness, callousness, faithlessness, and despair. However, Lamentations stands as a declaration of God's unwavering commitment to walk with us through our pain. It is a commitment that we can be grateful for and an invitation to walk authentically before him.

34

Listening: Our First Duty to God and Neighbor

One study on listening reveals that the average American's speaking rate is approximately 125 words per minute, while the human brain can process around 450 words per minute. Therefore, in a 5-minute conversation, you might speak roughly 600 words, but the listener can process up to 2200 words in that time.

It's no wonder many of us drift off when engaged in conversations and recall only 17-25% of what is said. Our minds have plenty of capacity for multitasking. Listening is indeed demanding and requires discipline. As Stephen Covey aptly notes, "Most people do not listen with the intent to understand; they listen with the intent to reply."

When we break it down, it becomes clear why listening is of profound importance and why the absence of it can be painful. Voice is a primary means through which we contribute, share, connect, and express our individuality.

Listening is a profound act of respect and honor, conveying, without words, "I value you. I see you. I care about you." Non-listening, on the other hand, communicates the opposite, and understanding this perspective helps us grasp why it can be so detrimental to individuals and teams.

Listening is challenging because it demands humility—it places others above us, requires us to suppress our desire to be heard in order to serve others, and positions us as learners. In the words of Doug Larson, "Wisdom is the reward you get for a lifetime of listening when you'd have preferred to talk." But wisdom is never easy to come by; it is a hard-earned prize. The best things in life are often found on the other side of hard.

Reflecting on my relationships, I've found that my most significant failures are often tied to non-listening. I am guilty of listening not to understand, but to reply. I am guilty of forming conclusions before gathering all the facts. When it comes to improving my listening skills, I welcome all the help I can get. Fortunately, Scripture offers abundant guidance and grace as we seek to become better listeners.

James emphasizes the importance of listening over speaking, recognizing our natural tendency to speak first: "Know this, my beloved brothers: let every person be quick to hear, slow to speak, slow to anger" (Jas 1:9). Proverbs 18:13 provides valuable wisdom on the subject: "If one gives an answer before he hears, it is his folly and shame."

This verse reminds us that rushing to speak without first listening can lead to misunderstandings, miscommunications, and even harm to relationships. In contrast, Proverbs 20:5 promotes the skill of drawing others out through patient listening and thoughtful questioning: "The purpose in a man's heart is like deep water, but a man of understanding will draw it out.

Dietrich Bonhoeffer, influential theologian and author, beautifully captures the significance of listening: "The first service that one owes to others in the fellowship consists of listening to them. Just as love of God begins with listening to his Word, so the beginning of love for our brothers and sisters is learning to listen to them." Here, Bonhoeffer draws a parallel between listening to God's Word and listening to one another. Both acts are rooted in love and are integral to building meaningful connections within a community.

Listening is an expression of love, honor, and respect towards others. It conveys authentic interest and genuine care for their thoughts, feelings, and experiences. When we truly listen to someone, we offer them the gift of our attention, making them feel valued and validated. In contrast, a failure to listen can lead to misunderstandings, strained relationships, and a sense of dismissal or neglect.

The art of active listening is essential in fostering empathy and understanding. It requires setting aside our own assumptions and preconceptions, humbly seeking to grasp the perspective and emotions of the speaker. By doing so, we create a safe space for vulnerability and open communication.

The act of listening goes far beyond the physical act of hearing; it is a profound expression of love, empathy, and respect. When we listen to God's Word and to one another with genuine attention and humility, we create fertile ground for meaningful connections and mutual understanding.

In a world often consumed by noise and self-centeredness, embracing the art of listening can be a transformative and deeply enriching practice. As we learn to listen, we participate in a dance of love and compassion that nourishes our souls and strengthens our relationships with both God and our fellow human beings.

35

Jesus is the Address of God

The word "fray" is a verb, signifying the act of unraveling or becoming worn at the edges due to constant friction. It also serves as a noun, defined as a battle or an intense conflict. This concept closely resembles life, at least in my experience.

Both the noun and the verb hold true. Life is a battle, and friction is common. It's not unordinary to find ourselves worn thin and exhausted. At times, we may feel like we are coming undone, unraveling; life can be quite messy.

The good news in all of this is that God inhabits both the verb and the noun. He comes to us at the edge and meets us in the chaos. He is no stranger to a war-torn existence, to sorrow, suffering, and death. He is worn by their edges. Jesus Christ is the embodiment of God.

In Christ, God makes his home with us. The Son of God "became flesh and blood and moved into the neighborhood" (Jn 1:14, The Message). The incarnation means that God has come to live with us in the fray.

To put it another way, Jesus is the address of God. Let me explain, but first, allow me to share a story. 39 Burnshirt Road is one of fifteen addresses we've called home. It was a stunning place to live, located in rural Massachusetts, surrounded by acres of forest and sitting beside a pristine lake. It remains our favorite place to live to this day. Its true beauty, however, was its residents

39 Burnshirt Road was a residential home for juvenile offenders. These young men would stay for 6 months to a year, earning their

GEDs, gaining a trade, developing life skills, and receiving spiritual nourishment. Our desire was to bring Christ to this place, so we moved to 39 Burnshirt Road. You can imagine our surprise when we learned that Christ was already a resident there.

I thought I was bringing him there, but instead, I found him there. I shouldn't have been shocked. He said we would find him in such places. "I was in prison and you came to me...whenever you did this to someone overlooked or ignored, that was me—you did it to me" (Matt 25:36, 40, The Message).

It's unmistakable. We find God where we least expect to find him. He's hidden in the stranger, the hungry, the thirsty, the naked, and the sick (Matt 25:34-40). Richard Beck, in his book "Stranger God: Meeting Jesus in Disguise," states, "We don't show hospitality to be like Jesus; we show hospitality to welcome Jesus. In Matthew 25, Jesus isn't the one doing the visiting. Jesus is the one being visited." I had it backward. 39 Burnshirt Road was Jesus' address. I was the guest.

God has a track record of living in unanticipated places. He lived in a tent for years, 440 to be exact (Ex 25-40; 1 Kgs 6). He passes by the proud while making his home in lowly, contrite individuals (Is 57:15). His people are his dwelling place. Though sinful, broken, and needy, he indwells us individually and corporately (1 Cor 3:16; Eph 2:22).

The first four books of the New Testament tell the story of God's greatest address change. God came to Earth. The Christmas season was moving season for God. The New Testament says that in Christ, we encounter "all the fullness of God in a human body" (Col 2:9, NLT). In other words, Jesus is the address of God.

The principle is critical to grasp. Where Jesus makes his home, God makes his home. If Jesus is at home somewhere, God is at home there. This is why we find God in the gutter, among the homeless, beside the widow, and with the broken. That's where Jesus calls home.

Jesus lives in the fray. He is in the mess. This is the best news. It means that God is down in the dirt with us. It also means we don't need to leave the mess to find him. In fact, we will miss him if we look for him anywhere but in the fray.

I Will Not Forget You

There I was, laid out on the ground while my wife held our newborn daughter, surrounded by nurses administering salts to revive me— not exactly my finest hour. Yes, I passed out during the birth of my fourth child. After enduring labor, my wife was fine, while I was the one collapsed on the floor.

Birth, with all its intensity, is an awe-inspiring experience. The weight of the moment is undeniable. Witnessing my wife cradling our newborn was a profoundly beautiful sight, a connection that felt like a divine lesson in itself.

In fact, it is one of the most profound and astonishing expressions of God's unwavering commitment to us is found in the context of the mother-infant relationship. The book of Isaiah contains a remarkable passage where God speaks tenderly to the exiled people of Israel, drawing a striking parallel between his love and that of a mother for her child.

God poses a rhetorical question, asking, "Can a woman forget her nursing child, that she should have no compassion on the son of her womb? Even these may forget, yet I will not forget you" (Isaiah 49:15). This comparison highlights the powerful and instinctual bond that exists between a mother and her child. A mother's love is often regarded as one of the strongest expressions of devotion, care, and compassion in human relationships.

However, the Bible remains rooted in realism, acknowledging that even the strongest human bonds may falter. It acknowledges that there are rare and unfortunate instances where a woman may forget her child or fail to have compassion for them. Despite the fragility of human love, God assures us that his love is unparalleled and unconditional.

In an astounding proclamation, God declares, "I will never forget you." His love transcends all human limitations and is immeasurably greater than even the deepest motherly love. Such is the depth and steadfastness of God's love for his people that it is incomparable to any other affection we may experience on Earth.

When we meditate on this divine promise, we are confronted with the enormity of God's love for us. As human parents, we may experience profound love for our children, but even that is but a shadow of the boundless love God has for each one of us. The love God offers is unyielding, unshakable, and everlasting.

If you are a parent, you can relate to the widening of the heart and the deep affection that arises when interacting with your own children. Yet, even in the depths of such love, we can still be overwhelmed by the unfathomable love and loyalty that God extends towards us.

This promise of being engraved on the palms of God's hands speaks to his unwavering care, protection, and remembrance of his people. It serves as a powerful reassurance that we, as God's chosen ones, will never be forgotten or forsaken. In moments of doubt or hardship, let us hold onto this promise and take it to the bank of our faith.

The love of God endures forever, and his commitment to us surpasses all earthly bonds. Fight to rest in the assurance that you are deeply loved, cherished, and remembered by the Creator of the universe. He will certainly not forget you.

Learning from the Weird Stuff in the Bible

The Bible holds some weird stories. J.B. Phillips captured it: "The Bible is not only strange; it is stranger than we can imagine." From tales of whales swallowing men to fiery chariots ascending to heaven, talking donkeys, plagues of frogs, rivers turning to blood, and bushes unharmed by flames, it's a mingling of unusual narratives.

The foundational creed of the Christian faith affirms the truth of these realities and essentially says: "You think that's strange? Listen to what I believe about God becoming man, born of a virgin in a humble stable, facing capital punishment of the time, and ultimately triumphing over death."

The story of Enoch stands out as one of these strange stories—he fathered the oldest recorded man, living an astonishing 969 years, and notably, he himself never faced death. It's undoubtedly an unusual narrative. However, within these stories, there exist valuable insights to be discovered, even in the most peculiar accounts.

Enoch's life presents us with an intriguing lesson, one that speaks to the profound impact of parenthood on our spiritual journey. He stands as one of the remarkable figures in history, a man who escaped the clutches of death, just like Elijah, and was taken by God from this earth (Gen 5:24). The defining characteristic of Enoch was that he walked with God, and this holds a significant lesson for us all.

In examining the short account of Enoch's life in Genesis 5:21-24, we discover a pivotal turning point. It was after the birth of his son Methuselah that Enoch began to walk with God. The event of fatherhood, the moment when he transitioned from a family of two to three, served as a catalyst for his spiritual transformation. Before that, was a time when Enoch did not walk with God.

Parenthood has a unique way of deepening our faith and drawing us closer to God. The responsibilities of being a parent forced Enoch to recognize his moral and spiritual limitations, compelling him to rely on God for help. The experience of inadequacy as a parent humbled him, leading him to lean on God for strength and guidance. Many parents can resonate with this sentiment, feeling the weight of responsibility driving them to their knees in prayer and dependence on God. I sure can.

The presence of children in our lives serves as a powerful purifying force. Just as our presence in their lives can have a holy influence on our children (1 Cor 7:14-16), their presence in our lives pushes us towards change. God has designed the family as a place of transformation, where the interactions, challenges, and joys of parenthood draw us closer to him.

As parents, we will find ourselves humbled, seeking God's wisdom, grace, and strength to navigate the complexities of raising children. In these moments of vulnerability and dependence, we learn to rely on God's unfailing love and guidance. Parenthood teaches us humility, patience, and the need for divine wisdom in raising our children.

In the midst of life's demands and responsibilities, God gently reminds us not to stand too long on our feet but to find strength on our knees. It's on our knees that the true wars are waged, battles fought, and God's intentions for our lives are worked out. In these humble postures, we experience his presence and power, transforming us into more dependent people.

Resilient Joy: Unmoved by Circumstance and Sorrow

Joy in this world must always be explored against the backdrop of sorrow. Paul describes life with the striking phrase: "we are sorrowful, yet always rejoicing" (2 Cor 6:10). The true surprise in this paradox is that joy can be present at all in a world so wracked with pain. How can it be? Doesn't pain push out joy? Where does a joy like this come from? How can it stand alongside sorrow?

Diving into the concept of joy, we discover that it is not rooted in circumstances; otherwise, it would cease to exist alongside sorrow. These passages are case in point.

- "The joy of the Lord is your strength" (Neh 8:10).

- "Well done good and faithful servant enter into the joy of your Master" (Matt 25:23).

- "That my joy may be made full in you" (Jn 15:11).

- "The Fruit of the Holy Spirit is...joy" (Gal 5:22).

Nehemiah 8:10 highlights that joy originates from the Lord himself, independent of external circumstances. In Matthew 25:23, Jesus speaks of entering into the Master's joy, emphasizing that joy is outside oneself and intimately connected to the presence and approval of God. John 15:11 points to an experience of Christ's joy, which is everlasting and complete. Galatians 5:22 lists joy as one of the fruits of the Holy Spirit, further underscoring that joy is a divine attribute.

Joy originates from God himself. Each text highlights the joy experienced by each Person of the Trinity, revealing that the joy of the Lord is the joy of the Father, Son, and Holy Spirit. Our God is the Triune God—a single eternal God existing in three distinct persons. Within this Triune community, joy exists in its purest form.

In the Trinitarian existence of God, joy finds its primary expression in mutual delight. Before the creation of the world, God's Triune existence was complete and satisfied. The three persons delighted in one another, loved one another, and shared true joy (Jn 1:18, 17:24).

Out of the overflow of their love and joy, creation came into being. Throughout the narrative of Scripture, we witness the bursting forth of this joy among the members of the Trinity: the Father delighting in the Son, the Son delighting in the Father and the Spirit, and the Spirit delighting in the Father and the Son.

The paradoxical intertwining of sorrow and joy is also rooted in the experience of God. In Christ, we see the fullness of God revealed. He embodies the God of joy, and yet he is also described as the "man of sorrows" (Is 53:3). In his life and ministry, we witness both rejoicing and weeping, celebration and lamentation. He perfectly exemplified the journey of being "sorrowful, yet always rejoicing" (2 Cor 6:10).

The experience of joy and sorrow is not limited to individuals but extends to the broader narrative of salvation history. The birth of Jesus Christ, as celebrated in the Christmas season, exemplifies the fusion of joy and sorrow. The arrival of the long-awaited Messiah brought great joy to the world, yet it also led to the massacre of innocent children by King Herod (Matt 2:16; Lk 2:10). The joy of Christ's birth coexisted with the sorrow of the brokenness and sinfulness of the world, highlighting the complex nature of joy in a fallen creation.

Moreover, joy finds its ultimate fulfillment in the redemptive work of Jesus Christ. Hebrews 12:2 reminds us to fix our eyes on Jesus, "who for the joy set before him endured the cross, scorning its shame, and sat down at the right hand of the throne of God." Jesus willingly embraced the cross, enduring immense suffering and sorrow, motivated by the joy of bringing salvation to humanity. His sacrificial act of love and the subsequent triumph of his resurrection bring hope and joy to all who believe in him.

From a theological perspective, the intertwining of joy and sorrow can be understood through the concept of the "already, but not yet." In Christ, we experience the "already" of salvation and the presence of the Holy Spirit, which brings joy even in the midst of today's pain. However, we also recognize the "not yet" aspect, acknowledging that the fullness of joy and the complete eradication of sorrow will be realized in the future consummation of God's kingdom.

We are invited to embrace both the joy and sorrow of our human experience. We are called to rejoice in the hope and promises of God, knowing that our present sufferings are temporary and that our ultimate joy is secured in Christ. At the same time, we are called to empathize with and bear the burdens of others, entering into their sorrows and extending the love and comfort of Christ.

Joy and sorrow coexist in the Christian. True joy is not dependent on circumstances but is rooted in God himself. It is a divine attribute expressed within the Trinity and extended to us through our relationship with him.

Through the life, death, and resurrection of Jesus Christ, joy and sorrow intersect in a profound way, offering us hope, redemption, and the promise of eternal joy in the presence of God. As we navigate the complexities of life, let us embrace the paradox of being "sorrowful, yet always rejoicing," finding solace, strength, and lasting joy in the Triune God.

Divine Proximity: Closer to God, Closer to Joy

Could a moderate climate and extended sunny days influence human happiness? This question was explored by researchers at the University of Vermont. Their findings revealed that "happiness rises and falls with distance from the equator," indicating that those living closer to the equator tend to experience greater happiness.

A similar study conducted by the Centers for Disease Control and Prevention, based on a survey of 1.3 million people across the country, supported these findings. It found that residents of sunny, outdoor-centric states like Louisiana, Hawaii, and Florida reported being the happiest Americans.

Conversely, the absence of sunshine often results in lower mood and diminished vitality. Research has shown that on overcast days, people are more prone to feelings of depression and irritability compared to the emotions experienced on cloudless days.

It makes sense that closeness to the sun correlates with better health. As someone who grew up in the Midwest and now resides in Florida, I wholeheartedly agree. I once spotted a bumper sticker on the road that brought it home to me: "Florida, because you never have to shovel sunshine." Closer to warmth, closer to flourishing and saying goodbye forever to snowy driveways.

This proximity principle also applies to our relationship with God. The Christian belief in the Trinity, the triune nature of God as Father, Son (Jesus Christ), and Holy Spirit, forms the foundation of the understanding that God is the source of all joy. The unity and relationship among the three persons of the Trinity demonstrate perfect love, harmony, and joy within the Godhead itself. This divine joy overflows and becomes accessible to humanity through our connection to God.

Throughout the entirety of Scripture, we find a recurring theme of joy being experienced in the presence of God. From the Old Testament to the New Testament, the significance of God's dwelling place is central to this concept.

In ancient times, the tabernacle and later the temple were symbolic representations of God's presence among his people (Ex 40:34). When these sacred places were built or rebuilt, there was an outpouring of joy and celebration, signifying the nearness of God to his people (2 Sam 6:14-17).

The book of Psalms, a collection of poetic expressions of worship and emotion, contains numerous references to joy, making it one of the most joy-oriented books in the Bible. Many of these psalms were sung in the context of temple worship, highlighting the connection between joy and the presence of God (Ps 47:2-3; Ps 122:1). Conversely, the book of Lamentations, written as a response to the destruction of the temple, reflects the deep sorrow that arises from the perceived distance between God and his people (Lam 5:15-22).)

In the New Testament, the incarnation of Jesus Christ, referred to as "tabernacling" or dwelling among humanity (Jn 1:14), represents the ultimate demonstration of God's desire to be with his creation. Jesus, being fully God and fully human, bridges the gap between divinity and humanity, bringing God's presence even closer to us. Moreover, through his death and resurrection, Jesus makes it possible for the Holy Spirit to indwell believers, making them the temples of God. This indwelling of the Holy Spirit within the hearts of believers is a profound expression of God's presence and leads to the experience of joy.

We live in a world marked by suffering, pain, and the consequences of sin. The human condition inevitably gives rise to sorrow in our lives. However, in these challenges, we find solace in the constant presence of God. The promise of Jesus' presence with us through the Holy Spirit reassures us that God will never forsake us (Jn 15:26-27). This assurance makes it possible for us to experience joy even in the face of adversity.

Paul beautifully captures this idea in one of his letters, where he writes from a prison cell, yet exudes joy: "Rejoice in the Lord always; again, I will say, rejoice" (Phil 4:4). Paul's joy is rooted in his profound experience of God's presence, even in the midst of difficult circumstances.

The concept of joy is inseparably linked to the presence of God. The Trinity, as the source of all joy, provides a foundation for understanding how our proximity to God influences our experience of joy. From the Old Testament to the New Testament, we see the pattern of joy being expressed in God's presence, whether through the tabernacle, temple, or the indwelling of the Holy Spirit in believers.

Despite the challenges and sorrows of life, the constant presence of God through the Holy Spirit enables believers to rejoice, finding joy in the assurance of God's unfailing love and his eternal dwelling among his people. With the psalmist, we can agree: "But as for me, the nearness of God is my good" (Ps 73:28). His nearness equals our joy.

40

If We Want to Get Wet, We Must Get into the Water

C.S. Lewis once said, "If you want to get warm you must stand near the fire: if you want to be wet you must get into the water. If you want joy, power, peace, eternal life, you must get close to, or even into, the thing that has them. They are not a sort of prize which God could, if he chose, just hand out to anyone." God is undoubtedly the source of joy, and through fellowship with him, we come to experience it as well.

Look at 1 John 1:3-4: "That which we have seen and heard we proclaim also to you, so that you too may have fellowship with us; and indeed, our fellowship is with the Father and with his Son Jesus Christ. And we are writing these things so that our joy may be complete." John proclaims the good news that connects people to the Triune God. It is through this message that fellowship with God is established. And it is in this fellowship with the Father and the Son that our joy finds completion.

In other words, joy is experienced through our relationship with the distinct persons of the Trinity. The gospel brings us the ultimate gift—God himself. The Father gives himself; the Son gives himself, and the Spirit gives himself. The fullness of God is graciously bestowed upon us through the redemptive work of Christ.

When we respond to God's action in our lives, we enter into a relationship marked by the grace and communion of the entire Trinity. As we engage with the Father, the Son, and the Holy Spirit, joy awaits us. This fellowship with the Triune God brings about a deep sense of joy that surpasses mere happiness or fleeting circumstances.

Paul provides further insight into the relationship between joy and the Trinity in Romans 15:13: "May the God of hope fill you with all joy and peace in believing, so that by the power of the Holy Spirit you may abound in hope." Here we discern the role of the Holy Spirit in producing joy in our lives. The Holy Spirit, who is a distinct person within the Trinity, fills us with joy and peace as we trust in God the Father. Through the power of the Holy Spirit, we can experience an overflow of hope, which leads to abounding joy.

Jesus also speaks to the connection between joy and our relationship with him and the Father in John 15:9-11: "As the Father has loved me, so have I loved you. Now remain in my love. If you keep my commands, you will remain in my love, just as I have kept my Father's commands and remain in his love. I have told you this so that my joy may be in you and that your joy may be complete." Jesus emphasizes the significance of remaining in his love and following his commands. By abiding in his love and living in obedience, we enter into a relationship that brings about his joy in us, resulting in the completion of our joy.

The New Testament reveals the dynamic of joy by emphasizing the importance of fellowship with the Triune God. Through the gospel, we are invited into a deep and intimate relationship with the Father, Son, and Holy Spirit. This fellowship with the distinct persons of the Trinity brings about the experience of God's joy. As we respond to God's grace and engage with the Father, the Son, and the Holy Spirit, we can experience a profound and lasting joy that surpasses circumstances and finds its fulfillment in our communion with the Triune God.

God is not secretive about accessing his joy. He is clear that joy is found in fellowship with him. It emerges as we connect with him, converse with him, listen to his Word, and engage with his people. When we unfurl the sails of our lives and let his divine wind catch us, joy finds us. God is not hiding; his arms are wide open, and his invitation to an ocean of joy is ours for the having. If we want to get wet, we must get into the water.

41

God's Word Does What it Says

The Word of God, depicted as fire, hammer, sword, mirror, lamp, seed, water, and anchor (Jer 23:29; Heb 4:12; Jas 1:23-25; Ps 119:105; 1 Pet 1:23; Eph 5:26; Heb 6:19), fulfills its intended purpose in each representation—be it illuminating, nourishing, purifying, stabilizing, or protecting.

As Isaiah proclaimed, 'So shall my Word be that goes out from my mouth; it shall not return to me empty, but it shall accomplish that which I purpose, and shall succeed in the thing for which I sent it' (Is 55:11). God's word unfailingly achieves what it proclaims.

Genesis 1-3 vividly portrays the remarkable power of God's Word. Regularly returning to these chapters nurtures a deep appreciation for the effectiveness of God's Word. Within this foundational text, we witness the Word's compelling impact. Discover within these chapters how God's Word accomplishes what it proclaims:

- God's Word creates "ex nihilo," out of nothing (Gen 1:3). Through his Word, God brings forth the entire cosmos into existence from nothing, displaying his supreme authority over all creation.
- God's Word transforms what he created (Gen 1:9-13). The powerful Word of God initiates the separation of land and seas and brings forth vegetation and life, shaping the world according to his divine plan.
- God's Word commands creation's participation (Gen 1:24). He invites his creation to work with him in the ongoing

process of forming the diverse creatures that inhabit the earth.

- God's Word divides (Gen 1:6, 14). He establishes boundaries and distinctiveness in his creation through the power of his spoken Word.
- God's Word pronounces good, not good, and evil (Gen 1:3, 13, 18, 21, 25, 31, 2:16-17, 18). His Word establishes moral distinctions, defining the essence of goodness and declaring his judgment upon disobedience.
- God's Word is omnipotent, immediately effecting his commands (Gen 1:3). There is no delay or hesitation between God's spoken Word and its fulfillment; it is all-powerful and certain.
- God's Word is artistic and creative (Gen 1:1-25). The diversity, wonder, and beauty in all of God's creation reflect his creative Word, which is never dull but vibrant and full of life.
- God's Word brings blessing and purpose (Gen 1:22, 28). Blessing, connected to vocation, empowers his creation to fulfill its intended purpose.
- God's Word engages in divine dialogue (Gen 1:26, 3:22). Within the Trinity, God converses and communicates, displaying the relational nature of his Word.
- God's Word bestows authority and power (Gen 1:28). Man, made in God's image, is given dominion over creation and a voice with significant impact.
- God's Word works and commands (Gen 2:3, 16-17). His Word initiates work and provides moral guidance and boundaries for humanity.
- God's Word warns and judges (Gen 2:16-17, 3:14-19). Disobeying and distorting his Word leads to severe consequences and judgment.
- God's Word offers hope and promise (Gen 3:15). Even in judgment, God extends his gospel word of mercy and ultimate victory through the seed of the woman.

Observing the Word of God in action should evoke profound emotions within us—confidence in his power, hope in his promises, fear of his judgments, joy in his blessings, and gratitude for his mercy.

When God speaks, things happen; his Word is always true and effective. Martin Luther reveled in this truth, expressing it vividly during his lectures on Genesis:

> *For if God can form a mass of water, call forth and create the heaven and its stars, each one of which equals or exceeds the earth itself in magnitude; if God can, from a small drop of water, create the sun and the moon, can he not defend my poor body against all enemies and against Satan himself? Can he not after that poor body is laid in the tomb raise it again to another and a new life? Wherefore we are to learn from this book of Genesis the power of God; that we may accustom ourselves to doubt nothing that God promises in his Word!*

This realization should significantly impact how we approach and handle Scripture in our lives. If we truly believe in the omnipotent, creative, and relational reality of God's Word, our lives will reflect that belief in action. A high view of Scripture should not be merely spoken but tangibly demonstrated through our deeds and actions. The power of God's Word is immense; our role is to position ourselves before it and allow it to work within us.

Vigorous, Brave, and Invincible: The Fruit of Assurance

The theologian and musician from the 1800s, Horatius Bonar, captures the crucial necessity of assurance in the fight of faith.

> *Uncertainty as to our relationship with God is one of the most enfeebling and dispiriting of things. It makes a man heartless. It takes the pith out of him. He cannot fight; he cannot run. He is easily dismayed and gives way. He can do nothing for God. But when we know that we are of God, we are vigorous, brave, invincible. There is no more quickening truth than this of assurance.*

Assurance ignites and fosters vitality—undoubtedly true. Discovering its source is paramount, this starts with acknowledging that it cannot be found within ourselves. Assurance in our faith is not derived from our own strength, faithfulness, or obedience, but rather from fixing our gaze on the activity and promises of the Triune God.

Our confidence is founded on the unshakable truth that nothing, in the most exhaustive sense, can separate us from Christ's love (Rom 8:38-39). The promise that nothing and no one can snatch us from the hand of God brings assurance (Jn 10:28).

The book of Jude beautifully reinforces this assurance through the theme of "keeping." Jude uses this language three times to emphasize the unyielding commitment of God to his people. At the beginning of the letter, he addresses his readers as those who are "kept for Jesus Christ" (Jude 1).

Then, in the heart of the letter, he exhorts believers to "keep yourselves in the love of God" while anticipating the mercy and eternal life promised by Jesus (Jude 20-21). Finally, Jude closes the letter by acknowledging God's power to "keep you from stumbling" and to present us blameless before his glorious presence with great joy (Jude 24-25).

The connection between God's choosing, loving, and keeping is inseparable. Those whom he loves, he keeps. Those whom he calls, he keeps. His keeping work assures us that we will persevere in faith until the end and stand before him without blame on the final day, filled with great joy.

Our role in this assurance is to actively participate in "keeping" ourselves in God's love. This self-keeping involves building ourselves up in the faith, praying in the Holy Spirit, and eagerly waiting for God's mercy at the return of Jesus. By consistently engaging in these practices, we abide in God's keeping love and deepen our assurance.

It is vital to recognize that God's keeping work is a Triune endeavor. The Father keeps us in and through Christ, and the Holy Spirit sustains us through prayer. Our focus on the gospel of Jesus Christ is a fundamental aspect of God's keeping. As we await Christ's return, the Triune God is actively at work, preserving us in his steadfast love and creating vigor, courage, and invincibility. He will keep you.

43

No Shadow and Not One Hint of Darkness

Shadows emerge when an object obstructs the path of light, preventing it from passing through. They represent darkened areas where the light source is impeded. Shadows surround us, yet they find no place near God. Described as the "Father of Lights" in whom "there is no variation or shadow" (Jas 1:17), light is his sole companion, making him the God beyond shadows.

Throughout the Bible, numerous "God is" statements invite us to explore his character. Verses portray God as love (1 Jn 4:8), faithful (1 Cor 10:13), a consuming fire (Heb 12:29), merciful (Deut 4:31), gracious (2 Chron 30:9), compassionate (2 Chron 30:9), and just (Ps 50:6).

One of the profound "God is" statements comes from John's first letter: "God is light, and in him is no darkness at all" (1 Jn 1:5). John emphasizes the absolute absence of darkness in God's character by using the double negative "at all." This strengthens the claim and highlights the impossibility of darkness residing in God. No darkness can taint his purity.

In the face of pain, suffering, and darkness we witness in the world, it may be tempting to question God's goodness. However, 1 John 1:5 stands as a resolute truth—God is pure light. This truth must shape our understanding of the darkness we encounter around us. In fact, he is the only reason we are not plunged into darkness. Karl Barth points out the grace of penetrating darkness, "In God, we find pure, undiluted light; his very essence is luminous, dispelling all darkness."

119

The gospel itself unfolds against the backdrop of light and darkness. Jesus' purpose in coming was to rescue us from darkness: "I have come as a light into the world, so that whoever believes in me should not remain in darkness" (Jn 12:46).

He identifies himself as the "light of the world," promising the "light of life" (Jn 8:12). At the cross, the world's darkest hour, the light of the world was extinguished so that we could be recovered "out of darkness into his marvelous light" (1 Pet 2:9).

Furthermore, John connects the divine luminosity to the pattern of Christian living. He urges believers to walk in the light as God is in the light. This call to walk in the light implies a life of repentance because the presence of sin is inevitable. Christians will inevitably stumble into darkness through sinful thoughts and actions. Acknowledging this reality is crucial to the Christian (1 Jn 1:6-9).

The distinguishing mark of a Christian is not the absence of darkness or sin, but the unwavering pursuit of the light and repentance. Christians recognize their own brokenness and refuse to remain in the darkness. Their aim is to walk in the light, which entails genuine confession, transparency, and surrender before the Creator. Hence Paul's reminder to those following Jesus: "For at one time you were darkness, but now you are light in the Lord. Walk as children of light" (Eph 5:8).

The God of the Impossible and the Laughter of Faith

Abraham, renowned for his unwavering faith, became a central figure in the Bible due to God's promises to him. The cardinal promise was that he would have a son, despite the apparent impossibility of it, considering his and Sarah's advanced age and her barrenness.

However, God delights in the absurd and revels in turning the impossible into reality. He calls us, like Abraham and Sarah, to have faith and trust in his promises, even in the face of circumstances that seem to contradict them (Gen 18:1-15).

Faith, as demonstrated by Abraham, is the laughter of trust in the face of the ridiculous. It involves moving away from self-reliance and looking toward God, recognizing our limitations and embracing his sovereignty. We abandon the notion that we can fulfill God's promises on our own and instead rest in his ability to accomplish the impossible (Matt 19:26).

Walter Brueggemann's Theology of the Old Testament provides further insights into Abraham's faith, which serves as a paradigm for the faith of Israel as a whole.

> *Israel has known ever since the barrenness of Sarah, that there is deep incongruity between the intention of God and the circumstance of lived experience. Israel, in the face of that incongruity, did not have many alternatives. It could accept the circumstance of its life as the true state of reality---thus for example, Sarah is barren and then the promise is voided within*

one generation. The alternative, Israel's chosen one in most seasons, is to rely on God's oath as a resolve to override circumstance, so that it is the promise and not the circumstance that tells the truth about reality. In this theological intentionality, Israel embraces this uttered testimony as the true version of its life.

The promises of God were abundant and far-reaching, intended to encourage Israel not to surrender to the grim circumstances of life, particularly when faced with deathly situations that seemed insurmountable. The incongruity between God's intentions and lived experiences was evident from the time of Sarah's barrenness.

In this context, Israel had two options: accept their present circumstances as the ultimate reality, leading to the nullification of God's promises within a generation, or rely on Yahweh's oath as a resolve to override their circumstances. Faith chose the latter, embracing God's promises as the ultimate truth about reality, regardless of the present difficulties.

Brueggemann's powerful phrase, "it is the promise and not the circumstances that tells the truth about reality," perfectly encapsulates the essence of faith. Faith is not about denying the dissonance between the promises of God and our present reality. It is about living in the tension between the two, affirming the certainty of God's promises and trusting in his timing for their fulfillment.

True faith seeks out the promises of God, meditates on them, clings to them, and triumphs over present circumstances through them. It acknowledges the reality of challenges but holds steadfast to the belief that God's promises will prevail. Faith, in this sense, becomes subversive of the present. It upholds the supremacy of God's promises over our current circumstances, refusing to let the latter have the final word.

As we learn from Abraham, faith teaches us to walk with God in the midst of life's uncertainties. It is an active, dynamic trust that shapes our outlook on life, leading us to believe in the reality of God's promises even when they appear distant or contrary to our experiences. Thus, we find strength, hope, and perseverance to navigate life's trials, knowing that God is faithful to his Word.

This is precisely what Paul emphasizes in the example of Abraham: "Without weakening in his faith, he faced the fact that his body was as good as dead—since he was about a hundred years old—and that Sarah's womb was also dead. Yet he did not waver through unbelief regarding the promise of God but was strengthened in his faith and gave glory to God, being fully persuaded that God had power to do what he had promised" (Rom 4:19-21).

45

The Privilege of Daily Labor and the Gift of Daily Bread

Work, eat, gym, sleep—the deployed military rhythm. Ask any deployed servicemember, and they'll confirm: it's a cycle, simple yet defining. The beauty of the deployed lifestyle is its inherent simplicity. Embracing minimalism, one leans into the simplicity of life and returns to the fundamentals.

This lifestyle serves many purposes, notably recalibrating one's perspective to the biblical essence of daily life. The Bible celebrates the sanctity of daily existence. It imparts wisdom, promises, directives, and tools to engage each moment in a meaningful way. It underscores the privilege of daily labor and the gift of daily bread, two things that define our existence.

Daily Labor. Work is undeniably a central theme in the opening chapters of the Bible. From the very beginning, we encounter a God who works, creating the heavens and the earth. As the narrative unfolds, we see that work is not only inherent to God but also a privilege given to humanity. Adam, the image-bearer, is placed in the garden to cultivate and care for it (Gen 2:15). This establishes the foundation for the significance of work in the human experience.

While work is initially presented as a gift, the curse in Genesis 3 brings forth thorns and thistles, making work arduous and toilsome. Despite this, Ecclesiastes sheds light on the paradox of work: "I perceived that there is nothing better for them than to be joyful and to do good as long as they live; also that everyone should eat and drink and take pleasure in all his toil—this is God's gift to man" (Ecc 3:12).

The book, often seen as a reflection on life under the curse, reveals the frustration and futility that can accompany human labor. The author bemoans the inability to fully determine the outcomes of one's toil, emphasizing the tension between effort and results.

However, even with the acknowledgment of life's uncertainties, Ecclesiastes highlights the divine perspective on work. He encourages embracing the gift of work joyfully, finding pleasure in toil, recognizing it as a gift from God. This perspective does not negate the challenges and limitations of work, but it points to a creaturely posture that acknowledges human dependence on God's providence.

Embracing work as a gift frees us from the burden of obsessing over the results. Each day becomes an opportunity to engage in the provision God has given us, fulfilling our responsibilities with dedication and love for God and our neighbors. Our jobs become a means to honor Christ and serve others, even when the desired outcomes may not materialize.

Viewing work as a gift enables us to find purpose and contentment in our daily tasks. We recognize that work is not solely a means to an end, but an opportunity to participate in God's ongoing creation and redemptive purposes. Our theology of work impacts how we approach our jobs, influencing the attitude, effort, and dedication we invest.

As we embrace work as a gift from God, we discover a deeper sense of meaning and fulfillment in our daily labors. This perspective challenges us to view our work as an act of worship, offering our best efforts to God while releasing the outcomes to his providential care. With this mindset, we can find joy and purpose in even the most mundane tasks, recognizing that our work is a means of glorifying God and serving others.

Daily Bread. Food serves as a reminder of our essential nature as creatures. Unlike our self-sufficient Creator, we are dependent beings, reliant on daily sustenance to continue living. This dependence points us to God, who graciously provides for our needs each day. The Lord's Prayer, taught by Jesus to his disciples, illuminates the importance of daily priorities in life and prayer. Within this prayer, we find a petition for daily sustenance, emphasizing the significance of seeking God's provision each day.

In both Matthew and Luke's versions of the Lord's Prayer, we encounter the plea for "daily bread" (Matt 6:9-13; Lk 11:2-4). This phrasing highlights the importance of acknowledging our daily need and seeking God's provision on a regular basis. Whether we're at the dinner table, going through a drive-through, or buying groceries, these moments call us to pause, appreciate, and enjoy the daily gift of sustenance.

Ecclesiastes echoes this sentiment, encouraging us to embrace the present and fully enjoy the daily provision amidst life's uncertainties: "Go, eat your bread with joy, and drink your wine with a merry heart, for God has already approved what you do" (Ecc 9:7). The author emphasizes the goodness of eating, drinking, and finding satisfaction in our toil, recognizing these pleasures as gifts from the hand of God. The anxieties of tomorrow should not hinder our engagement with the present; instead, we should relish the current provision and be fully present in the moment

Each morsel of bread becomes an invitation to recognize our creatureliness and give thanks to our Creator. It serves as a daily reminder of God's faithfulness and provision in our lives. When we embrace this truth, our worries about tomorrow diminish, and we find contentment in the present moment. Just as the Israelites received manna daily in the wilderness (Ex 16:35), we too are reminded of our dependence on God's daily provision and the freedom of living in the present with gratitude.

Food is a gift that not only nourishes our bodies but also connects us to the goodness and faithfulness of God. As we partake of our daily labor and bread, let us pause, give thanks, and be fully present in the moment, trusting that our God will continue to sustain us day by day. Allow each day of work and each meal we eat to become an opportunity to deepen our relationship with the Creator, embracing the dailiness of life with gratitude and joy.

46

Today's Trouble Meets Today's Mercy

Mark Twain quipped, "It ain't those parts of the Bible that I can't understand that bother me, it is the parts that I do understand." He wasn't wrong. The Bible is brutally honest, showing life as it is and will be.

Trouble is one of those unavoidable realities it talks about, much like Twain pointed out. As the book of Job says, "man is born to trouble as the sparks fly upward" (Job 5:7). While trouble is a certainty, so is mercy. Grasping this collision of daily trouble with daily mercy is helpful.

Daily Trouble. Anxiety is a prevalent issue that Jesus addresses. To illustrate its futility, Jesus employs examples from nature, such as birds, grass, and flowers, which do not worry about their needs being met. He emphasizes that anxiety is unproductive, yielding nothing of value while exacting a heavy toll on our well-being (Matt 6:25-34).

One of the core reasons why anxiety is futile is that it adds hypothetical troubles to the real challenges we face in the present. In essence, it burdens us with problems that may never come to pass. Jesus, in his teaching, urges us not to be anxious about tomorrow, as tomorrow will have its own challenges to contend with. He succinctly advises, "Sufficient for the day is its own trouble" (Matt 6:34).

The wisdom behind this instruction is profound and multifaceted. Firstly, it imparts to us the gift of biblical realism. Just as we expect daily sustenance through the prayer for daily bread, we must also anticipate daily troubles. This biblical realism grounds us in the reality of human existence, where trials are an inherent part of life.

Secondly, Jesus' teaching serves as an admonition against bringing tomorrow's worries into today. It encourages us to embrace the present moment fully and entrust tomorrow's uncertainties to God. By doing so, we acknowledge our dependence on God's provision and care, and we find peace in knowing that he holds our future in his hands.

Indeed, the path of wisdom is to engage fully with the challenges of today while leaving the concerns of tomorrow to the sovereignty of God. We recognize that the troubles of today are sufficient in themselves, and we need not add the burden of hypothetical anxieties to our plate.

Daily Mercy. Though daily trouble is certain, so are the necessary resources to engage it. While life may be fraught with grief and pain, there is a glimmer of hope shining through the darkness in the book of Lamentations: "The steadfast love of the Lord never ceases; his mercies never come to an end; they are new every morning; great is your faithfulness" (Lam 3:22-23).

In our suffering, we can find confidence in the assurance that God's love and mercies are unending and fresh every morning. These mercies are not a one-time gift but are continually renewed, demonstrating God's unwavering commitment to us, The text explicitly promises that God will pour out daily grace upon us, even in our daily troubles.

Imagine waking up each day with the knowledge that God's mercies are specifically designed for that moment. His love is steadfast, and his faithfulness knows no bounds. Regardless of our struggles, we can find strength in the fact that God is ever-present and attentive to our needs. As we entrust our worries and anxieties to him, we can rest in the assurance that his grace is more than sufficient for whatever challenges lie ahead.

The psalmist echoes a similar sentiment: "For his anger is but for a moment, and his favor is for a lifetime. Weeping may tarry for the night, but joy comes with the morning" (Ps 30:5). This psalm assures us that although we may endure sorrow and weeping during the night, joy will come with the morning. It echoes the sentiment of Lamentations, emphasizing the cyclical nature of God's mercies, where his favor and joy replace sorrow and mourning. The morning serves as a reminder of God's faithfulness and the hope of a new day filled with his kindness.

The Word of God acknowledges the certainty of daily trials but promises the assurance of daily mercy. Each new day presents an opportunity for God to fulfill that promise, meeting our needs and fortifying us to confront any challenges ahead. We can rest assured that as we journey through life, God's unfailing love and faithfulness will chase us down at every turn.

47

The Gospel's Power to Fulfill
Its Own Demands

When Paul wanted the church to preach the gospel, he preached the gospel to the church. His letter to the Romans teaches us many valuable lessons, including the passion Paul had to bring about the obedience of faith among all nations.

His desire was to take the gospel to places where Christ had not yet been proclaimed, and he sought the support, participation, and partnership of the churches he planted in fulfilling this mission. To achieve this, the church needed to be united in the gospel, recognizing that the same message they were called to preach over others was the very message that would unite and strengthen them.

Paul's unwavering conviction in the sufficiency of the gospel was evident. He emphasized the paramount importance of the gospel in every aspect of life, teaching the believers in Rome that it had the power not only to save them but also to set them free and compel them to reach the lost.

Paul understood that the gospel should shape their approach in engaging with those who have not yet heard the good news. Ultimately, the purpose behind it all was to bring glory to the Triune God as the gospel spread and the nations responded in faith.

In writing to the church in Rome, Paul had multiple objectives in mind. He aimed to foster unity among the believers for the sake of the nations, all for the glory of God. Remarkably, Paul's strategy for accomplishing this was profoundly simple: "I am eager to preach the gospel to you who are in Rome" (Rom 1:15). He recognized that the gospel is sufficient to produce what the gospel requires.

Scripture further illuminates the power and significance of the gospel. In Romans 1:16, Paul boldly declares, "For I am not ashamed of the gospel, for it is the power of God for salvation to everyone who believes, to the Jew first and also to the Greek." Here, Paul underscores the unmatched power of the gospel to bring salvation to all who believe. This affirmation reinforces Paul's unwavering confidence in the sufficiency of the gospel and its ability to accomplish its intended purpose.

Additionally, Jesus commands his disciples to proclaim the gospel in Matthew 28:19-20: "Go therefore and make disciples of all nations, baptizing them in the name of the Father and of the Son and of the Holy Spirit, teaching them to observe all that I have commanded you." This Great Commission echoes Paul's passion for reaching the nations and highlights the essential role of the gospel in fulfilling this divine mandate.

Paul's letter to the Romans teaches us the profound significance of preaching the gospel and its power to bring about the obedience of faith. Paul's own eagerness to proclaim the gospel to the believers in Rome reflects his unwavering conviction in its sufficiency.

As we embrace the centrality of the gospel in our own lives and share it with others, we participate in the larger purpose of bringing glory to the Triune God. The gospel is not only sufficient to accomplish what it requires but also to transform lives, unite believers, and propel the mission of reaching the nations.

48

Fighting for Our Lives through the Lord's Prayer

Prayer has been likened to a "wartime walkie-talkie," and in the case of the Lord's prayer, that description fits perfectly—it is a warrior's prayer. Jesus highlights the numerous dangers that surround us, emphasizing the need for honed situational awareness.

Once he recalibrates our hearts to shift focus from making our own name great and building our tiny kingdoms, urging us instead to relinquish our will in favor of aligning with his name, reign, and will, he then reveals the other threats we must combat daily.

Threat 1: Self-Sufficiency. The petition, "give us this day our daily bread" (Matthew 6:11), addresses our basic physical needs and reminds us of our dependence on God as our provider. Beyond mere sustenance, this plea also reflects our reliance on God for every aspect of our lives. We are not self-sufficient; rather, we need God's continual provision and care to navigate through each day. Daily bread reminds us that it is he who creates and sustains us, "not we ourselves" (Ps 100:3).

This request echoes the Israelites' experience in the wilderness, where God provided daily manna to meet their needs (Ex 16:14-15). Like the manna, God's provision is sufficient for the present moment, inviting us to trust him for what we need today, without being burdened by worries about tomorrow. Self-dependence poses a genuine threat, one that necessitates embracing the gift of our existence as creatures and the humility that accompanies it.

Threat 2: Unforgiven Sin. The prayer continues with "forgive us our debts, as we also have forgiven our debtors" (Matt 6:12). Here, we acknowledge the very real and persistent threat of sin and our ongoing need for forgiveness and mercy.

Matthew employs the language of debt in another passage, illustrating this principle through the parable of the unforgiving servant. This servant, forgiven an insurmountable debt, yet unwilling to release others from much smaller debts, is detailed in Matthew 18:21-35.

This prayer is closely linked, both conceptually and semantically, to that parable. It vividly illustrates our significant need for debt release and underscores the importance of extending that forgiveness to others. Unforgiveness is our default.

Martha Kilpatrick captures it well, "We are all on a life long journey and the core of its meaning, the terrible demand of its centrality is forgiving and being forgiven." This starts with pressing upward into the light and owning our darkness before God. It then moves outward to others and extends that undeserved light to others.

The movement toward forgiving can be painful. While we hope for mercy when we wrong God, we often desire justice for those who have damaged us. C.S. Lewis isn't wrong: "Everyone says forgiveness is a lovely idea, until they have something to forgive."

And yet, the horizontal dimension of forgiveness is intricately linked to the vertical—it's "as" we forgive our debtors that we receive forgiveness for our own debts. Put simply, they are interdependent—a person forgiven by God will, in turn, release the debts of others. One who refuses to forgive does not know forgiveness.

Threat 3: Temptation. The prayer addresses another potential danger, urging us to seek God's guidance to "lead us not into temptation, but deliver us from evil" (Matt 6:13). Sin is always "lurking at the door" (Gen 4:7), and temptation is its bait. James tells us: "Each person is tempted when he is lured and enticed by his own desire. Then desire when it has conceived gives birth to sin, and sin when it is fully grown brings forth death" (Jas 1:14-15).

Temptation is the prelude to sin, not sin itself. Understanding the distinctions and process James describes is crucial in comprehending the gravity of temptation, its eventual consequences, and the necessity of resisting it with God's help. Martin Luther speaks to the unavoidable nature of temptation: "Temptations, of course, cannot be avoided, but because we cannot prevent the birds from flying over our heads, there is no need that we should let them nest in our hair."

The plea of the Lord's Prayer for divine leadership emphasizes our reliance on God's wisdom and strength to resist temptation. It prompts us to acknowledge our limitations, the fragility of our wills, and our susceptibility to doing things we wish to avoid (Rom 7:16). In short, it fosters the humility and dependence necessary to wage war on all that leads us away from Christ.

Threat 4: Evil. The Lord's Prayer concludes with a final request that recognizes the ongoing spiritual battle we face: "deliver us from evil" (Matt 6:13). In the gospel of Matthew, the language of evil is used to describe threats within ourselves and external to us.

For example, "out of the heart come evil thoughts, murder, adultery, sexual immorality, theft, false witness, slander" (Matt 15:19). We are the threat. Essentially, the Lord's Prayer asks God to rescue us from ourselves.

The external evil envisioned here is the work of the enemy. The phrase "deliver us from evil" can also be translated as "deliver us from the Evil One," pointing to the reality of Satan's dangerous schemes. Satan seeks to steal, kill, and destroy—unraveling us, destroying our faith, crushing our families, and dishonoring God in the process. This is why Jesus prays that the Father would "protect them from the Evil One" (Jn 17:15).

This prayer makes us aware that we are unable to withstand the assaults of the Evil One without help. It points us to our need for a champion, a deliverer, a Savior. The Lord's Prayer is not the prayer of the self-sufficient but of those who know they need to ask, seek, and knock. It is the prayer of the poor in spirit, the mourners, the meek, and those who long to do what God requires but recognize they do not have the resources to make it happen.

In essence, the Lord's Prayer offers a comprehensive framework for confronting the significant threats we encounter. Through this prayer, we confront self-sufficiency, unforgiveness, temptation, and evil. It directs us to the Divine Warrior who combats our adversaries and equips us entirely for the struggle. With God's aid, we wield this weapon and fight with the support of heaven behind us.

Not Explaining Pain, Enduring It

"Jesus wept," these two words encapsulate a profound truth that changes our understanding of God. They reveal that God is not a distant and unfeeling deity but a compassionate and empathetic Savior who enters into our pain and grief.

In the face of human suffering, he does not turn away; instead, he absorbs it. Jesus' tears at the tomb of Lazarus show us that God hurts, God grieves, and God weeps (Jn 11:35). This is a revolutionary concept—our Creator is not immune to the sorrows of his creation.

Those who know the compassion of Christ toward them are called to reflect it. Paul urges us to "weep with those who weep" (Rom 12:15). To truly embody the compassion of Christ, we must be willing to walk the road of pain with those who suffer. At its core, compassion involves sharing in someone's suffering, embracing their pain, and accompanying them through their darkest moments.

Stanley Hauerwas adeptly emphasizes this when discussing the fitting stance for Christians in the face of evil—advocating for a pastoral approach over a philosophical one.

> *For the early Christians, suffering and evil . . . did not have to be "explained." Rather, what was required was the means to go on even if the evil could not be "explained"—that is, it was important not to provide a theoretical account of why such evil needed to be in order that certain good results occur, since such an explanation would undercut the necessity of the community capable of absorbing suffering.*

This touches the core issue: how do we authentically support each other in the face of pain? Words and answers can only serve a suffering individual to a limited extent. Embracing a limping friend, walking alongside them, sharing their sweat, pain, and tears, while acknowledging our lack of answers together—that is a completely different story.

Dr. Alan Wolfert, founder of the Center for Loss, introduced the model of grief engagement known as "companioning," which offers valuable insights and resonates deeply with the biblical spirit of compassion. At its core lies humility—an approach to supporting sufferers that strives to do no harm. He presents eleven guiding principles for compassionate engagement.

1. Companioning is about being present to another person's pain; it is not about taking away the pain.
2. Companioning is about going to the wilderness of the soul with another human being; it is not about thinking you are responsible for finding the way out.
3. Companioning is about honoring the spirit; it is not about focusing on the intellect.
4. Companioning is about listening with the heart; it is not about analyzing with the head.
5. Companioning is about bearing witness to the struggles of others; it is not about judging or directing these struggles.
6. Companioning is about walking alongside; it is not about leading or being led.
7. Companioning is about discovering the gifts of sacred silence; it is not about filling up every moment with words.
8. Companioning is about being still; it is not about frantic movement forward.
9. Companioning is about respecting disorder and confusion; it is not about imposing order and logic.
10. Companioning is about learning from others; it is not about teaching them.
11. Companioning is about compassionate curiosity; it is not about expertise

This approach embodies compassionate action—it exemplifies what we seek when we ourselves are in distress. In times of pain, we don't desire to be fixed, patronized, lectured, or misunderstood. Instead, we want people to be present to us, to step in and shoulder the weight of sorrow, to refuse answers, and to just walk with us. It moves away from explaining pain to enduring it, together.

Cutting through the Fog to the Shore

Florence Chadwick, the first woman to swim the English Channel both ways, ventured in 1952 to swim from the Catalina Islands to California—a 26-mile distance. Despite the foggy and cold weather, she swam for 15 hours straight, barely able to see the accompanying boats. Exhausted and cold, she was surrounded by nothing but fog and decided to quit, telling her mother aboard one of the boats.

Her mother encouraged her, saying the shore wasn't far. Despite this, Chadwick stopped. Moments later, she realized the shore was merely ½ a mile away. Reflecting on it at a news conference the following day, she said, "All I could see was the fog... If I could have seen the shore, I believe I would have made it."

As the certainty of the cross drew near and his disciples felt fear, Jesus comforted them, saying "Do not let your hearts be troubled." He continued, saying:

> *You believe in God; believe also in me. In my Father's house are many rooms. If it were not so, would I have told you that I am going there to prepare a place for you? And if I go and prepare a place for you, I will come back and take you to be with me so that you also may be where I am (John 14:1-3).*

The antidote for troubled hearts lies in God's promised future. The strength needed to persevere comes from a clear vision of what lies ahead. By fixing our gaze on God's assurance of a certain future, we pierce through life's uncertainty and fog. The Bible affirms that seeing the destination keeps us moving forward—our hope for the future fuels our endurance through our present struggles.

Revelation 21 offers the most vivid portrayal of the shore in Scripture. Written for believers enduring considerable suffering, pain, temptation, and persecution, it speaks to their agony and provides them with a needed glimpse of the shoreline. What does God speak into their pain? What does he speak into ours? He reveals the home he's preparing, the final destination awaiting us.

Then I saw a new heaven and a new earth, for the first heaven and the first earth had passed away, and the sea was no more. And I saw the holy city, new Jerusalem, coming down out of heaven from God, prepared as a bride adorned for her husband. And I heard a loud voice from the throne saying, "Behold, the dwelling place of God is with man. He will dwell with them, and they will be his people, and God himself will be with them as their God. He will wipe away every tear from their eyes, and death shall be no more, neither shall there be mourning, nor crying, nor pain anymore, for the former things have passed away." And he who was seated on the throne said, "Behold, I am making all things new." Also, he said, "Write this down, for these words are trustworthy and true" (Rev 21:1-5).

Four points can be taken from this passage: the promise of a new earth, the promise of a new city, the promise of God's presence with us and the promise of the God's removal of pain.

The Promise of a New Earth. Heaven is not where you will spend eternity. Michael Wittmer's opening line in his book, on eternity—"I don't want to go to heaven, I want the earth"—certainly grabs your attention, especially in a book about heaven written by a Theology Professor.

When thinking about your eternal future, how do you perceive it? Is it filled with excitement or boredom? Do you envision a spiritual existence without a body, featuring harps and clouds? Do you think of it as a never-ending church service or an eternal sing-along in the sky? If that's the prospect—I'm in agreement with Professor Wittmer.

However, that's not the case. The passage guides us to our ultimate destination. Heaven isn't our final home—the earth is. Imagine being on a plane and someone asks where you're headed—you don't mention the layover city, but rather the location where your travel ends. Likewise, the earth is our final destination; heaven is a layover.

The thrust of the New Testament hope is resurrection. Certainly, upon death, believers go to heaven with God, which Paul assures us is a far superior state than our present one. However, a missing element remains until Christ's return: the restoration of our bodies and the creation of a new earth.

You were not made for heaven; you were made for earth. We were formed from the dust of this earth, from its soil, and thus, we are intricately connected to this place. Our affinity for the earth we inhabit is deeply ingrained within us.

We rightly love our walks on the beach, the sand between our toes, the taste of lemonade, the hug of a child, the sound of a beloved tune, the sight of a mountain, the cool breeze on our faces, the taste of ice cream, and the warmth of a familiar friend. We cherish these tangible gifts—these earthly realities.

Are we going to lose all these things in the future? The answer is a resounding no. Our physical existence wasn't our design; it was God's idea—he deemed everything he created as good in Genesis 1-2. The descent into sin ushered in a curse that ruptured all things, yet God's design is restoration. What he originally labeled as good isn't discarded—instead, he restores, redeems, and renews (Is 65:17, 66:22; 2 Pet 3:13).

Many have often claimed, and I've said it myself, that out future with God exceeds our imagination, and lies beyond our comprehension. Yet, this verse seems to challenge that notion, suggesting that we can indeed envision it. Considering we're destined to reside on a new earth, isn't it reasonable to draw some ideas from our current earthly experience? While the glory of this new earth will undoubtedly surpass our perceptions, we still possess a framework to comprehend our eternal home.

The Promise of a New City. This promised city is unlike any other—it's likely the very place Jesus promised to prepare for us. Within its walls, the city signifies God dwelling among his people, fostering a profound sense of community. It's destined to be the greatest of cities, marked by perfect unity within unparalleled diversity. Imagine a community where people from every tribe, tongue, language, and nation contribute to the vibrant culture.

Will singing be part of our worship in the new earth and within this new city? Absolutely, it's inevitable—our joy will overflow. Yet, worship encompasses far more than song; it involves service, labor, creativity, education, exploration, and savoring all that God has crafted. The rest of Revelation 21 indicates that nations will bring their distinctive glory into this new city. The New Testament uses language like ruling, serving, and learning to illustrate our future—a progression of what God originally intended for us, not a limitation of our humanity (Rev 21:22-27).

The abilities you've longed to cultivate, the passions you've yet to pursue, the friendships awaiting deeper connection, the destinations you've dreamt of exploring—these will materialize in the new earth. The vision of Revelation 21-22 dismisses the notion of a mundane future and illuminates the extraordinary life that lies ahead.

The Promise of God's Presence. From Eden, where God walked among his people, to the wilderness where he dwelled in a tent, and in Israel within the tabernacle, God's presence was tangible. In Christ, God drew nearer than ever before, walking among his people, and through the Spirit, he dwells within them. God has always fervently desired to reside with us, but this is an unprecedented scenario—the Triune God establishing his throne permanently on earth—Father, Son, and Spirit dwelling with us eternally.

This forms the essence of what makes a place home. Martin Luther once remarked, "I would rather be in hell with Christ than in heaven without him." It is God's presence that truly defines the new earth as home. Home transcends being a mere location; it's a relationship.

Ultimately, our deepest longing isn't just for God's gifts but for his presence—to behold his face, walk with him and worship him, share meals, and abide in his company. Jesus will be present in bodily form—we will see, touch, walk, and embrace him. In his presence, we will find our true home.

The Promise of God's Removal of Pain. Revelation 21 contains the most cherished promise—one that assures the complete eradication of suffering, sin, and pain. It's the wiping away of "every" tear—every ounce of pain healed, every mourning consoled, and every physical hurt repaired. It guarantees with absolute certainty that tears of sorrow will never fall again—the only tears from your resurrected eyes will be those of eternal joy... endlessly... forever. This signifies the comprehensive eradication of all pain.

Though sorrow may last for the night, joy comes with the morning. And in this place, the sun never sets and morning never ends (Rev 22:5). You're not in the final chapter of your journey; this is merely the preface. Your current pain won't dictate the conclusion. God, the ultimate healer, promises a future with him devoid of pain and sorrow.

Too Good to Be True? The passage concludes with a fascinating statement about the reliability of everything previously conveyed—I find this deeply comforting. It demonstrates how well God understands us. He knows that it all sounds too good to be true. He knows that our pain is substantial and that expecting hardship is more familiar to us than anticipating joy. That's precisely why he assures us.

Every word about that promised future is "trustworthy and true." God never utters falsehoods; the Bible explicitly states that he "cannot lie" (Num 23:19)—it's an impossibility (Heb 6:18). If you've placed your trust in Christ, remember, he assured that he's preparing a place for you. He said, "I would not have told you this if it were not so" (Jn 14:1-2)

Consider the compassion and understanding in Jesus' words—it's as though he's communicating, "I would never treat such significant matters lightly; I would never mislead you or say such things if they were not true. I couldn't do that to you. You can trust me."

This is the battlefield where faith operates—it clings fiercely to these incredible promises, fighting for even a glimpse of the shore. It clings to what God has said, steadfastly rejecting the current reality in favor of his promised future. It stays in the ring, embracing the gospel in the present moment, trusting what he declares true about us even when our experiences seem contradictory. My dear friends, put those fists up and never stop swinging.

Milton Keynes UK
Ingram Content Group UK Ltd.
UKHW051003120124
435908UK00012B/98

9 798869 083890